A JOURNE
CHALLENGES, HC. _, ...

59
PRIME

MICHAEL K. FRANCIS

59 Prime: A Journey of Faith, Challenges, Hope, and Triumph

Copyright © 2021 by Michael K. Francis
ALL RIGHTS RESERVED. No part of this book may be reproduced or transmitted in any form or by any means, electronic or mechanical, including photocopying, recording, or by any information storage and retrieval system, without written permission from the author, except for the inclusion of brief quotations in a review. For permissions, contact Michael at Michael@59prime.com

Publication date: December 2021

ISBN Print: 979-8-9851452-0-5
ISBN eBook: 979-8-9851452-1-2

Library of Congress Control Number: 2021923882
1. Inspirational   2. Motivational   3. Memoir   4. Life Lessons
5. Self Help   6. Personal Development
I Francis, Michael K. II *59 Prime: A Journey of Faith, Challenges, Hope, and Triumph*

59 Prime may be purchased at special quantity discounts for industry-related businesses as well as U.S. trade bookstores and wholesalers. Contact Michael at Michael@59prime.com

Cover, Layout, and Design: Megan Leid
Editor: Mel Cohen
Publishing Consultant: Mel Cohen of Inspired Authors Press LLC
   inspiredauthorspress.com
Contact Michael for Rights or Licensing Agreements:
   Michael@59prime.com
Publisher: BEAM Publications
Website: www.59Prime.com
Printed in the United States of America

TABLE OF CONTENTS

ACKNOWLEDGMENTS

Mine has not been a solo expedition. There have been many incredible people who have helped me navigate life's crevasses, including: My parents: Marshall Lanier and Charles Etta Francis. My partner of 35 years in life, love, and adventure: Janel Sylvia Jefferson

My brothers: Elton "Tweety" Ray, Anthony "Tony" Lanier, and Brian Earl Francis. My sister-in-law, Marilyn Joyce McKenzie Francis, for providing constant emotional and spiritual support

My in-laws: Leroy Augusta and Jean Maudry Jefferson*

My sister-in-law, Cheryl Jean Jefferson, for articulating my personal thoughts and experiences

My family, by blood and marriage

My mentors: My Dad, Lori Johnston, Brian McNamee, Ted Bagley, Sam Wood, and Patti Boyle. *Thank you.*

My lifesavers: Alan Gorn, MD, Rheumatologist (Los Angeles), Brock Harper, MD, Rheumatologist (Austin), Timothy McNicoll, MD, Family Practice (Simi Valley, CA), William Stivelman, MD, Ophthalmologist (Thousand Oaks, CA), and Ryan Young, MD, Ophthalmologist (Austin). *Thank you.*

My "go-to crew": Ken Bigham, Mindy Bloomberg Binder, Alton Boriack, Joseph Brown, David Byrd, Tanya Currie, Shivie Dhillon, C. Renee Dobson, Ashley Eddington, Tecuan Flores, Chris Fong, Cullen Harris III, Robert Hawkins, Ted Hazen, Darren Holmes, Stephen Janda, Chester Jones, Sharon Wallace Jones, Paul Ksiazek, Marc Lujan, Ken Moris,

Michael Murguia, Jason Nolte, Eric Ofosu Obeng, Rose Rivera, Mark Sanders, Thomas Sanders, April Zanelli Solie, Michael Tapscott, Leslie D. Thomas, Doug Wilson, and Vennard Wright. *Thank you.*

My "long haul" high school and college friends, of which there are hundreds

My global trekking companions: Dan Fowler, Maggie Villarreal, Helene Barrette, and Paul Montenegro

My professional colleagues, now considered life-long friends. Among them: Michael Abramovitz, Kasey Adamchik, Sharon Agnew, Paul Aguilar, Steven Aguilar, Tami Aguilar, Quionna Allen, Kim Allred, Gretchen Alva, David Anders, Chon Asuncion, Mary Atwood, Wesley Au-Yeung, Robyn Babcock, Heather McGaugh Ball, Bob Baltera, Michael Baram, Lindsay Barnett-Kaplan, Alice Barriciello, Jennifer Michel Beachler, Elliot Beimel, Chip Bell, Jim Benes, Jean Berry, Steve Bertram*, Cedric Betts, Don Bitner, Lisa Orbin Boecker, Brent Brightwell, Liz Browning, Amy Jun-Bruno, Scott Buck, Peg Bundgaard, Glenn Burchard, Laura Burns, Jeff Burton, Candice Callahan, Chai Cai, Kim Camacho, Jennifer Hampton Campbell, Steve Canepa, Kathryn Cannone, Lindsey McDermott Cantu, Kelly Cassidy, Ruby Castillo, Caroline Chan, Socar Chatman-Thomas, Som Chattopadhyay, Glen Choi, Jim Cochrun, Annie Coleman, Brenda Coleman-Beattie, Edda Colon, Ruth Cotter, Tracy Curran, Tanya Otterbein Currie, David Dart, JoAndi Depew, Etheline Desir, Kiersten Geary DiChiaro, Ernest Donkor, Vanessa Downey-Little, Duane Doucette, Patrice Dudley-Aviles, Kristen Early, Sam Ellis, Candy Emerson, Erin Emmer, Marc Fields, Hugh Fischer, Kelly Fisher, Diana Flores, Sylvia Flores, Mike Fontes, Andrew Fox, Pat Gallio, Robert Gama, Thomas Garrett, Heidi Germano, Terri Gibbons, Sonja Glatzhofer, Dollie Grajczak,

Cathy Gust, Kristi Meyer Hamilton, Trent Hamilton, Chris Hawkins, Dale Herron, George Hertzberg, Katie Himes, Debbie Holler, Kevin Hornish, Matt Hostetler, Laura Hrabovsky, John H. Hudson, Sandy Calderon Hughes, Joy Avery Hunt, Jack Huynh, Vivian Ikupolati-Adeniyi, Jamie Karpilow, Arun Kochhar, Amie Krause, Andre Jackson, Andrew Jacobus, Rose Jennings, David Johnston, Samin Joshi, Mary Kennett, Bernie Knobbe, Valerie Kroenke-Aguilar, Steve Leach, Niles Lichtenstein, Galen Lim, Pamela Reed-Litten, Alex Lopez, Trish Lovering, Blake Lowry, Zoe Philippides Lundberg, Kayla Jordan Mahdavi, Simon Martin, Chau Mai, Ted Mayorga, MyVan McLay, Robert McLennand, Alfredo Mendez, Anthony "Tony" Mitchell, Ron Myers, Carole Heinze Mendoza, , Nancy Mhatta, Solange Mikita, Brian Miller, Derek Miller, Nicole Miller, Jeff Minyard, Perwez Moheet, Larysa Mysyk, Ginny Napoli, Jeff Naven, Susan Andrews O'Neal, John Oakes, Joe Parise, Jennifer Parsons-Kerr, Mark Pearson, Deanna Pendrick, Del Peterson, Shawn Pixley, Anton Rabushka, Fletcher Ramirez, Chris Rei, Bill Rich, Bev Richardson, Courtney Rogers, Jill Rogers, David Rosales, Angie Rosenthal, Gabriel Rueda, Treva Rumbeck, Jennifer Sandoz, Loredana Santelli, Mark Schneider, Karen Schenk, Chin Boon Seng, Magdalena Rosa Serrano, Bonnie Shenkman, Lori Silver, Paul Simoneau, Jessica Wolf Simpson, Ray Skidmore, Michelle Smith, Bryan Song, Joah Spearman, Ahsok Srinivasan, Kim Steele, Dennis Stern, Bill Stott, Kathryn Sutton, Kay Tanner, James "J.T." Taylor*, Liz Arevalo Tepezano, Eduardo Torres, Christopher Todd, Stuart Tross, Tanya Turner-Fields, Ian Twohig*, Martin Van Trieste, Cecile Tu, Nassera Vezelis, Alan Waldman, Brigitte Walker, Sara Wasson, Joe Weber, Scott Whelan, Kim Williams, Chris Wingert, Demet Yalcin, David Yapp, Nadia Younes, Gerald Youngblood and Adeel Zaidi

My "inner circle" neighbors in Texas and California

My Accountability Coach, Kim Nugent, EdD, for providing invaluable feedback and guidance throughout my journey. *Thank you.*

My editor and publisher, Mel Cohen (Inspired Authors Press), for creative insights, copy editing, and unwavering support throughout the dynamic publishing process. *Thank you.*

My graphic designer, Megan Leid (Designs by Day Star), for meticulously editing and proofing my ramblings and eloquently creating and illustrating my vision for *59 Prime*. *Thank you.*

My website designers, Carol and Jeff Stec (Tylerica Systems), for creating an incredible platform to share *59 Prime* with the world.

* Forever missed, but watching from above

PREFACE

I believe that there is something extraordinary about the number 59. Not just because I turned 59 in January of 2021, or because I randomly selected the date range of February 1-March 31 to compile inspirational, career, and life quotes—a range of precisely 59 days. 59 was unique long before fully revealing itself to me. Its claim to fame is attached to an effective date for 401K retirement withdrawals. 59 is also a powerful arithmetical value with tentacles, character, and substance. It is an irregular prime, a safe prime, and the 14th super-prime—nothing is divisible by 59 but 59.

I have always associated the definition of "prime" as being the best example of an optimal situation, a unique point in time in one's life, or an inflection point. But now, after turning 59, it possesses a new, more profound meaning to me. Now, it is a reflection point in my life, complete with vivid examples, a plethora of reminders abruptly polished with humbling moral undertones.

This compilation recaps my life observations, challenges, and triumphs. I am who I am because of the unique relationships, events, and experiences, both good and bad, that have burnished my armor and strengthened my core. The time is finally right to share these precious gems given to me during the past 59 years.

I wrote *59 Prime* after realizing that I have been guilty of forgetting about some of the significant life obstacles that I have overcome, but more importantly, some of the personal growth commitments made in the midst of them. So, from now on, *59 Prime* will be a reminder to me now and a resource in the future whenever the next wave of life's storms arrives.

A gift is not a gift if it is linked to reciprocity, praise, or pronouncement. True gifts are given from the heart, with love and silence. At the point of exchange, ownership transfers immediately from the giver to the receiver. So now, at 59, I humbly invite you to open, partake, and hopefully choose to share what I've learned. Whatever you decide, please know that these gifts now officially belong to you. In closing, if you take but one pebble from my battered but now fortified shore, always remember, there are better days ahead.

Gratefully Yours,

Michael K. Francis

DEDICATION

This book is dedicated to my big brother, Elton Ray Francis. He departed far too soon but left an enduring legacy and blueprint on living life to the fullest. Fifteen years after gracefully stepping off life's track, we continue to draw upon your courage, compassion, strength, and random acts of kindness. Especially today, in these challenging times, your gifts illuminate a noble yet humble path forward. Even though you are gone, your authentic presence remains a constant source of motivation and inspiration. Love you always and forever.

FOREWORD

When we think about what it means to be blessed, most of the time, we think about the good things happening to us. But what about the really difficult times that we sometimes don't understand, like a financial setback, an unfair situation at work, a divorce, the loss of a loved one, or an unexpected illness? In the case of Michael K. Francis, I feel blessed—as a friend and business colleague—to have participated as a passive observer and prayer partner as he journeyed for 59 days through an unprecedented Texas ice storm, an unexpected health challenge, a near-death experience, and the loss of his eyesight. I had the good fortune to watch as Michael emerged from darkness to light, from limited vision to seeing clearly again, from extreme physical health obstacles to unwavering faith, belief, clarity, and knowing that better days are ahead.

59 Prime is the outpouring of Michael's thoughts, inspirations, and reflections of his life well lived as he observed and contemplated his life's ups and downs. He used this challenging time as an opportunity to grow and knew he was not in this dark place by accident. His faith and positive perspective moved him through this valley of despair. Michael summarizes 118 (59 X 2) thoughts and observations he learned as he navigated through these troubled waters in *59 Prime*. His talents and gifts from his successful professional career, passion for food and music, and love and service to all were revealed to him in vivid color.

This book is a must-read for anyone who finds them-selves in a challenging time in their life. It is filled with wis-dom, insight, motivation, and optimism to not only help you survive but to thrive. After the unprecedented Texas ice storm, the trees in our yards looked weak, like they had wilted and died. Yet now, three months later, they have straightened back up, are filled with leaves and flowers, and are stronger than ever. Like the trees, the same is true for each of us. When you emerge from one of life's storms, you will be stronger, healthier, wiser, better off, and ready for new growth and opportunities if you keep the faith and a positive perspective.

In my bestselling book, *Transform Your Job Search, Turning Fear into Opportunity*, I dedicated Chapter 3 to very troubling and difficult times in my life. The chapter's title, *The Dark Night of the Soul*, is not unique to Michael and me. When we read the accounts of all the great poets, mystics, and writers throughout all of humanity, we recognize this is all a part of our life journeys. These episodes in our lives are a time to grow and connect to our highest potential. When we look back on these experiences, no matter how great the loss, we see that these times didn't happen to us; they happened for us.

—By Patti Boyle
Friend, Business Colleague, Amazon Bestselling Author, Award-Winning Entrepreneur, International Speaker, Facil-itator, and Transformational Business Coach

As one of only two African-American Executive Directors of a state agency in the State of Texas, I am uniquely aware of what leadership and challenges look like. Being black and leading a predominantly white organization in a red state requires various skills, tolerance, resilience, and support. It is not a one-person show. It is a vision-focused, team-driven, daily existence.

I was fortunate to have been the youngest of four sons born into the Charles Etta Jackson and Marshall Lanier Francis dynasty. They created a safe space in the south in the sixties for four boys of color to experience patience, grow in confidence, learn the love of family, and exercise compassion. These lessons were planted, watered, and nurtured in faith. Our parent's love story is the birthplace of my courageous warrior, friend, and big brother Michael Francis. And now, he is a safe space for family and friends in a chaotic world.

Michael is a thoughtful leader with a humble touch. He has a story—or more accurately, a perspective—within his journey that is inspiring and instructional. I have had the blessing of a front-row seat to the healing power of hugs, humor, and kindness. Clearly, I am biased, yet it doesn't make it any less accurate. My vantage point allowed me to witness my brother nurture his leadership and life philosophy through some incredible peaks and disturbing valleys. His storms have been literal, physical, emotional, and professional. And yet here he is—wiser, kinder, and more grateful for each storm. In fact, he would be the first to tell you, "Someone always has it worse than you, Brian." He believes this and lives it daily.

The following pages provide a glimpse into what grace looks like in the face of adversity. My brother Michael has always walked with a sense of peace and concern. Peace within himself, and respect and concern for others. As I read this book, his words are a cathartic gift to us. I couldn't wait to turn the page to the next lesson and the next nugget of wisdom, with tears inevitably rolling down my cheeks because I know his story. I know his struggles. His words spoke a bridge over my difficult times. His wisdom and insight are universal.

59 Prime is a personal perspective for a diverse audience—businesswomen, single dads, aspiring leaders, struggling sons and daughters, and those that have lost their faith. *59 Prime* is for you. It is a penetrating look into the human spirit and its capacity to see the best of this world in the worst of our moments. It reminds us that goodness and humility are powerful gifts when wielded by open hands and from an open heart. *59 Prime* is the calm we all need to help us weather our next storm. I can't wait for you to turn the page.

—Brian Francis
Brother, Executive Director at Texas Department of Licensing and Regulation, Career Mentor, Author, Poet, Human Rights, and Trafficking Advocate

CHAPTER 1

MY ROOTS

"If you know where you are from,
it is harder for people to stop where you are going."
—*Matshona Dhilwayo*

My name is Michael Keith Francis. My parents, family, and friends call me "Michael" or "Mike." For some reason, probably because after 40-plus years, I think of her more as a sister than a sister-in-law, Marilyn calls me "Mikey," and is the only person allowed to do so. By any standard of measure, I am an average person, one of four boys born in the late 1950s to early 1960s. We were fortunate enough to have been blessed with exceptional, hardworking, and loving parents. As of this writing, they have celebrated 63 incredible years together.

I am the third eldest, the entire gang sandwiched by age into a five-year window. Elton and Tony are older, and Brian is younger. This narrow timeline made it easier for my parents to corral us, allowed for consistency in discipline, and optimized the four-tier hand-me-down system. We thrived in what I now fully appreciate and acknowledge as an environment based on an overabundance of food, family, support, and love. Each sibling was outgoing in their unique way: some instinctively engaged overtly, and others (mainly me) preferred to operate covertly, even today. At times, I find it interesting that I'm considered outgoing and loquacious by most people's standards. But I guess it's all relative, no pun intended. Some people find it hard to believe when I tell them, "Seriously, I'm the quietest one in the bunch."

Reflectively, I was and currently remain the unofficial family nerd—a term I now respond to proudly with a small but humble dose of genuflection. We are different yet the same, especially when it relates to family, integrity, injustice, and inclusion. I often say, "We are cut from different parts of the same cloth."

When you are born into a nurturing, supportive, and loving family, especially in your preadolescent years, you tend to take what is normal for granted and don't realize how unique your family core is until others applaud or crave access. Even today, friends I have not seen or heard from in decades remain close to my parents. If you had the opportunity to meet them, they would quickly become compassionate shoulders, your extended family, and "back-up parents" in some cases.

I am proof that it does take a village to raise you. Or at least, it helps to have a slew of fully invested and nurturing aunts, uncles, and cousins. My mom is one of five siblings, with two sisters and two brothers. My father is one of nine, with three sisters and five brothers. They were born and raised in the 1940s just outside the small town of Giddings, Texas, which I jokingly refer to as a big metropolis (population 5,000). Segregation was in full effect when they grew up. However, not a single memory they shared contained a trace of hate, anger, or resentment. Knowing what I do now, I have even more respect for their resilience and commitment to diversity and inclusion. They remain perpetual guiding rays of light for me and many others. Always amazing, inspiring, and notorious for providing random acts of kindness, shelter, and love.

We couldn't wait to see each of our cousins during our preteen years and spend our summer vacations in Texas at our maternal grandparents' (Charlie & Frankie B. Jackson) house. They lived about six miles outside of Giddings, or as we used to say, "out in the country." Their dog, Sport, would jump off the front porch and welcome us home.

Their home had no plumbing; you did your business in the outhouse! There was no air conditioning, just mesh screened sliding windows with strategically placed box fans. If you got cold, be careful what you asked for, they'd put heavy quilts on you that would restrict your ability to breathe or move. We all bathed in the kitchen in galvanized steel tubs and drank rainwater from an old tin cistern on the side of the house.

Our grandmother would get up early, and we would awake to the smell of pan-fried Hormel summer sausage (the one with the round black peppers in it), scrambled eggs, and homemade biscuits with some Delta or Brer Rabbit syrup (for sopping, with a bit of butter mixed in there). Ummmmmpf!

While that house is no longer there, the love and memories that we shared as a family continue to connect and ground us. We are truly blessed.

I remember my dad telling me about his tour of duty at Ramstein Air Force Base in Germany. His brother—my Uncle Sutton—had already been stationed there for a year, and made sure his younger brother would hit the ground running. Before arriving, Uncle Sutton had Dad's transportation, off-base housing, and, more importantly, his food connections in order.

And Francis family reunions, well, let's say they are tough to beat. Never in your life will you hear more laughing and lying, eat until you are as full as a tick on a whale, or experience so much hugging and kissing that your entire body will be sore for days. What a wonderful feeling!

Who could have known those insightful, off-the-cuff phrases and antiquated tales from my Aunt Cee, Aunt Babe, and my Uncles Joe, Sutton, and Forest, would have tangible, real-life, and corporate world application. They have also strengthened and reinforced the connective tissue for future generations. Their words were always powerful and continue to reverberate at family gatherings, but their actions were where the rubber hit the road.

My DNA

Our first cousin relationships are abnormal in the best way possible. We possess similar and notable family features and traits: our walk, hugs, laughs, and genuine love of food, especially fried. We are more united, supportive, and loving than most siblings. Frequently, we gather, encourage, mentor, celebrate, and grieve together as a family. While some families might look for ways or reasons to be apart, we aggressively create excuses and seek opportunities to be together. Our DNA instinctively informs us that each Francis family gathering will, by default, be memorable, epic, energizing, and potentially the last for anyone of us. So we leave nothing to chance, nothing unsaid, and nothing on the playing field, knowing that our light will eventually dim.

I have been provided with precious and unique DNA strains that allow me to:

1. Intuitively throttle up or down to meet any moment like my mother.
2. Remain calm, stay grounded, be logical, and keep things in proper perspective like my father.

These are the most valuable traits my parents—Charles Etta Jackson and Marshall Lanier Francis—bequeathed to me:

From my mom: compassion, dedication, energy, flexibility, honesty, outreach, and perseverance.

From my dad: analytics, drive, discipline, focus, honor, planning, and wisdom.

From both of them: confidence, faith, family, food, love, optimism, and work ethic.

These traits are an integral part of my core and, along with my collective life experiences, make me who I am. I chose to embrace a slightly above-average and optimistic perspective on life and prefer to believe that optimism, hope, and a few real-world examples might be just the antidote to lift someone up or to be a catalyst for others to share their life story. I know my journey only scratches the surface of what millions have (or are going) through. No one gets out of this thing called life unscathed, so each of us has a unique story to tell. One that might help or inspire others to persevere. Why not share your secret recipe on how you made great lemonade from a bushel of lemons. Life lessons are potentially more valuable to the living.

Your DNA determines your physical features—eye and hair color, height, size of your nose, and so much more. I am one of many paternal relatives with careers in (or who possesses a strong aptitude in) mathematics, accounting, finance, and analytics. I chose to believe that my grandfather, Professor George Franklin Francis, would bequeath that expertise to his descendants through complex algebraic calculation or maybe just by fate. However it occurred, it is firmly encoded into our DNA. Understanding your past allows you to calibrate and better prepare for your future.

About ten years ago, the light finally came on for me. I'm aging, so that means my parents are aging, and the world is aging. While I remember bits and pieces of my family history, there was no cohesive, validated, or formal family manuscript for current or future reference. I should have documented and archived conversations instead of just listening to my grandparents, aunts, and uncles. Unfortunately, as each generation transitions and leaves this existence, so do more intricate pieces of an already complex and scattered puzzle. My analytical side wanted to know more about my ancestral history and lineage, and I knew just who to turn to (again).

As usual, my incredible wife Janel was way ahead of me in her historical preservation and genealogical quest. Nevertheless, I leveraged her knowledge and tips on how best to reconstruct my history. I immersed myself into the exciting, never-ending, and often sobering journey of understanding **MY ROOTS**. But I quickly learned, be careful what you ask for, and brace yourself for a rollercoaster ride that summits with glorious peaks and plummets into deep, dark valleys.

For most African-Americans, conducting genealogy is just outright challenging because of enslavement. As a race, our ancestors were programmed to endure a lot over the centuries and say even less about it. As a result, most of what is shared about the lives of our ancestors, especially before the 1930s, is a watered-down version of the actual events and circumstances. Even today, much of what transpired remains hard to comprehend and just too painful to relive or recite. But we all must stare directly into it and call it for exactly what it is and remains: WRONG. Otherwise, we give it the power to evolve with times and reemerge in more covert and more acceptable ways, shapes and forms.

So under the watchful eye of slave owners, we developed our way to communicate, celebrate and commensurate African-American history. Gospel music and Divine Providence were critical pillars that supported our plight. Gospel music evolved into one of the primary mediums for us, as a people, to express our sorrow, hope, resiliency, pain, suffering, and faith. Singing was one of the few freedoms my ancestors had permission to do without fear, intimidation, or retribution.

Those old Negro spirituals remain a powerful and inextricable part of our American history, tragically vetted by centuries of blood, sweat, tears, and broken promises. Today, some of those same plantation songs, now more than three hundred years old, are solemnly sung and hummed in churches and homes across our nation. Those sacred and precious hymns continue to serve as a constant beacon about faith, unity, and modern-day aspirations for a better life.

Here is a deeper look into the ethnical side of my DNA and roots. I am a formulaic genetic blend originating from:

6% Hispanic ancestors from Mexico/Spain/Portugal
5% Caucasian ancestors from England/Wales/North Europe
89% West African ancestors from Nigeria (47%), Cameroon (20%, Bantu), Benin & Togo (13%) and Mali (9%).

I am incredibly proud of the 89% West African DNA coursing through my veins. **MY ROOTS** directly link to the Nigerian, Cameroon, Mali, Benin, and Togo regions, and I descend from the Bantu tribes/people. Three of my great-great-grandparents were captured, enslaved, and brought from West Africa to North and South Carolina, most likely during the 1700s at the peak of the transatlantic slave trade. Between the 16th and 19th century it is estimated that 10 to 12 million enslaved Africans were transported across the Atlantic Ocean. My ancestorial tree includes surnames of Francis, Mitchell, Jackson, Garcia, Moody, McCoy, Booker, Arnolds, Nunn, and Thomas from these origins.

I am also incredibly proud of the 6% Spanish and Hispanic DNA coursing through my veins. My great-great-grandfather, Benigno "Ben Benita" Garcia, came to Texas from San Miguel de Allende, Guanajuato, Mexico, in the late 1850s. Ben was the son of Jorge and Florentina Molina Garcia, my great, great, great grandparents born around 1815. Ben bought land and settled near Sequin, Texas. He fell in love with a slave, Sarah "Belle" Gordon, whom he purchased and quickly married, taking her out of bondage. Their marriage was officially recognized on October 9, 1865, in Seguin, Guadalupe County, Texas. From these origins, my ancestorial tree includes the surnames of Garica, Sanders, Thomas, and Molina.

However, I am not as proud of the 5% Northern European DNA coursing through my veins. This strain is most likely the result of unspeakable sexual atrocities committed by a slave owner (or other opportunists) against my innocent female ancestors. In the 1700s and early 1800s, Census and Property archives confirm that slaves and families were frequently sold, killed, and separated. Thus, even if recorded and logged in journals, my early ancestors remain mostly unnamed except for any identifying scars or tribal markings and subsequently counted along with the slave owner's livestock. My origins from these ancestors may never be known due to the circumstances surrounding their unwanted intrusion into my family tree.

Researching my ancestry has been an ongoing journey, with many incredible discoveries and a few gut-wrenching twists and turns. To date, I have identified over 3,100 direct ancestors and have been able to identify fourteen of my sixteen great-great-grandparents born in the 1820s and 30s. Although some were married for decades, none were "officially" recognized as husband and wife, or more than three-fifths of a person until word of their freedom from enslavement (The Emancipation Proclamation signed on January 1, 1863) finally reached Texas on June 19, 1865 (aka Juneteenth). For perspective, most Americans of European descent can trace their roots to the 1700s with minimal research and a lot further with some assistance. But things are what they are, and I will continue to explore **MY ROOTS**.

Sadly, our country continues to struggle with racism in part, I believe, because shining a bright light on the past casts a dark shadow on what our nation is supposed to stand for. It is hard for me to understand, so I know it must be even harder for some to admit or accept it. But just because you don't want to talk about or acknowledge something doesn't mean it did not happen or will be forgotten. On the contrary, I believe quite the opposite is true because there is a strong correlation between denial and reoccurrence. History ignored is history repeated. Take a look around if you need proof.

In the end, I am thankful for each day in my 59 years of existence and for the many burdens my parents, relatives, and ancestors bore on my behalf. Time is a precious and non-refundable commodity. Millions of people are only here for a short duration but have left poignant and permanent footprints. We are all playing life's game against an unknown but ticking clock and against an undefeated foe: TIME.

Reflectively I see that my life experiences over the past 59 years helped shape my perspectives, and ultimately, my choices. My evolution has occurred primarily on big "Aaawh, hah!" moments coinciding with pivotal life events or while slowly transitioning from one generational milestone to the next. Life does not linger just because we choose to.

Just so I'm clear. I've made quite a few bad choices and asked for forgiveness, and had to course correct many times in my life. But we learn, grow, and evolve, always and without end, unless we choose a stagnant alternative, where no change = NO CHANGE.

My Parents

I am a military brat. Growing up in the military allowed my parents to shield us from much of the harshness that still exists in the world today. With each location change, we were forced to start anew, build friendships, and learn more about different cultures, people, and ultimately ourselves. Growing up on a military base, race, color, and religion was irrelevant, or at least not something that trickled down to children. Our network and our home were a melting pot of diversity. It wasn't until I turned 14 and my father retired from military service that we moved back to Texas permanently. We began to take note of occasional racial slurs, the true reason for some of the railroad tracks and what it meant to "stay on your side of the tracks," and discriminatory undertones, all due to our skin color.

Our parents taught us that people are people, regardless of race. Therefore, you cannot characteristically classify a person based on race, ethnicity, religion, or other discriminatory hurdles. We are all individuals; a better barometer of character is to watch what people do. Actions speak louder than words. In the end, we quickly resolved not to let anyone change who we engaged with or how we would be defined. To this day, that's how we roll!

My father joined the US Air Force in 1955, retiring 20 years later as a Tech Sergeant. Military service was a way for a young black man to achieve a better life and show society that we were willing to serve our country despite the social circumstances. Remember, honor, drive, work ethic, and discipline are some of his DNA attributes. We were so proud of our dad and how he moved up through the ranks. Last summer, while visiting my parents, I found four albums filled with hundreds of awards, pictures, and recognition certificates for his exceptional service, leadership, and several technical process improvements. For him, he was following a long legacy of Francis men and women who have proudly served our country. To date, 24 relatives have taken the oath to serve and protect our country —one of them making the ultimate sacrifice.

On June 5, 1917, at the age of 24, our great-uncle, Clinton Francis from Giddings, Texas, enlisted in the United States Army. In 1918, from February 19 to October 24, Pvt. Francis served overseas in Company D in the 509th Engineers Service Battalion. Unfortunately, like thousands of other service members fighting in Europe, he contracted tuberculosis. Pvt. Francis was quickly dispatched back to Camp Mills on Long Island, New York, but died shortly after returning on November 24, 1918, at 25.

Even while in service, the long tentacles of racism were present. In the early 70s, my father was stationed at Mountain Home AFB in Idaho. We looked forward to the drive back home to Texas to spend the summer with family and friends. Mom would fry up a bunch of chicken for the trip, all four of us boys would jump into the Ford Fury III, and we'd make the 3-day road trip, occasionally stopping along the way to sightsee and explore different parts of the country. At night, our whole family would sleep in the car at roadside parks. Brian, being the smallest, would crawl up and sleep in the back window. What a blast, what great memories!

My heart sank decades ago when dad told me, "Son, your mom and I tried to make sure those trips were special, despite all the racial problems that were happening to us as a people. We wanted to protect our children because you didn't ask to be here." He said, "Even though I was in the military and even if I identified myself as such, we weren't allowed to stay in any hotels along the way because we were black. Me and your mom, well, we always tried to make the most of any hand we were dealt. You can't change the cards, so you have to shuffle them around and look at different options."

Sometimes, to not speak of a thing condones it and allows it to be repeated. George Floyd was one of the thousands who have suffered injustice. Unfortunately and fortunately, it was captured, shared, and documented for the world to see. In the absence of cell phones, there is a high probability the whole story and truth would remain untold and no one charged. Long after the end of slavery, our government has some unfinished atonements to acknowledge publicly. It has not protected all of its citizens or treated them equally. Removing these events from educational curriculums will not remove them from history. The way I was raised was that if you did something bad, especially if you were in a position of authority, you owned up to it. You admitted it was wrong, identified viable solutions, and did not repeat it. It's called integrity. It's time for the United States to do the same.

Dad retired in 1975, and we returned to our parents' roots in Giddings, Texas. Throughout our military travels, this was where we always spent our summer vacations. So it was a "coming home" of sorts. We had friends and knew there would be lots of good food and more family gatherings.

You'd be hard-pressed to find a more loving and nurturing person than my mom, Charles Etta Jackson Francis. She has been the calming soul and vocal prayer warrior within our family during life's storms. I'm not sure what I did to deserve being her son, but I am grateful every day.

She's a diminutive and beautiful woman, standing a mere 5 feet, 3 inches, with an adjustable presence that immediately fills an entire room with spirituality and kindness. Her feet are tiny, her cadence quick, and her steps are huge. Her faith has been shaped by the hands of time, and she's covered some very tough terrain. A lot of it on behalf of others, myself included. She is hard to keep up with, but will stop on a dime for anyone in need.

She can be found bouncing around the house, perpetually multitasking while humming gospel favorites, stopping periodically to take a phone call (after locating the phone), or making one to someone that just popped into her mind. She just had to let them know they've been on her mind, and she is praying for them. These "just in time" interventions happen at least a dozen times a day and can even interrupt a nap if that's when she feels that call of duty.

I have heard her lovingly called "Mom," "Momma Charles," "Aunt Charles," "Charles Etta," "Lou Baby," or "Mrs. Francis" by hundreds of souls. My parents have always made their house a home to anyone in need. It wasn't until Covid-19 that my parents started locking the front door during "unofficial" business hours. There was always a steady stream of family and friends dropping by, so there was no need to keep it locked, especially when a simple, "Come on in, it's open!" would suffice. I finally received my house key in 2020.

There is rarely a day that goes by without us having a conversation. I know that we are on the downside of our time together. So I try to create, capture and relish every moment possible. I know her presence will always be with me regardless. She has taught me a lot about faith, life, sacrifice, and death. But just in case, I have kept all the voicemails she has left me, so I can replay her saying, "Hey baby, it's your mom. I hope you are having a blessed day. Give Mom a call when you get a chance; I love you, Pookie."

MY BEGINNINGS

During my high school sophomore year (1977), I began to think about my future and realized everything hinged on financial independence. First, I needed to get a job. So that summer, I applied for a Shift Cook position at the local drive-in. Unfortunately, I was too young, six months shy of the minimum state employment age requirement. During the job application conversation, I quickly pivoted and struck a deal with the manager to buy me some time and show my DNA-gifted work ethic. I asked him, "How about if you let me maintain the drive-in's lawn for $15 per service every other week for the next six months?" Done! So my first official job was "Landscaper," and six months later, I was hired as Shift

Cook. I was right about financial independence—the tradeoff was responsibility, but I'd been taught that all my life. I've been making contributions to Uncle Sam and Social Security for the past forty-three years, so I can say with a high degree of conviction that work is overrated and quite frequently gets in the way of my life.

At the drive-in, I worked two days during the week and one on the weekend. After school, the bus would drop me off at home. I would grab my work clothes and then walk 1.5 miles to work using the backstreets in whatever crazy weather Texas decided to have that day. My dad would pick me up around 11:30 pm, and I would be up at 6:30 am for school the next day. Rinse, repeat.

Two months after my promotion to cook, I opened a checking and savings account at the local bank. Then in August of 1978, as the new school year started, I could buy my clothes, which gave me freedom. For Christmas that year, I surprised my parents with a forty-eight-piece dining set, which they still have some forty-three years later. The look on their face and the feeling that, in some small way, I was helping and providing some return on the investment they had made in me was priceless.

In 1979, I was a junior in high school. So I set up a meeting with a counselor to discuss my post-graduation plans. I confidently informed him that I planned to take the ACT and attend a 4-year college or university and major in Business Administration with a focus in Finance to leverage my grandfather's DNA gifts. After I finished articulating my plan of action and professional aspirations, he calmly asked me, "Michael, have you ever thought about just going to a trade or vocational school? There's a really good one in Waco (Texas)".

I graduated in the top 25% of my class and was also an accomplished track athlete. As a senior, I competed at the state meet as a member of the 400 meter relay and individually in the 200 meters. I placed second in both events and attended Southwest Texas State University (aka Texas State University) on a full track scholarship. I finished with that Finance degree and went on to get my MBA. I have held Finance, Accounting, and Human Resource roles in both the municipal and federal government. I have also held several senior-level positions at four Fortune 500 companies in four different industries. Currently, I am the Founder of BEAM Executive Advisors, providing a hybrid of Management Operations and Human Resource consulting services. I selected the name "BEAM," not just for Webster's definition:

(a): a ray or shaft of light,
(b): to smile with joy,
(c): a directional flow of particles or radiation,
(d): a ship's breadth at its widest point.

It is also a constant reminder of my foundation, my parents, and the work ethic they instilled in us. The official date of LLC licensing by the state of Texas is September 17, 2020— my oldest brother's Elton's birthday. BEAM stands for **B**rian, **El**ton, **A**nthony, and **M**ichael.

Forty years later, I'm proud I had the courage and confidence back then to ignore that counselor's words and not let his advice give me cause to doubt myself. To some people, what I and many others wanted to accomplish was considered abnormal for African-Americans back then. But the concept of higher education was not foreign to me because of how I was raised and my lineage. Through words and actions, my parents made us realize that we were capable of whatever we wanted to achieve in life. Never let someone else set the height of your bar.

The moral of the story: regardless of who you are, prepare yourself for success, plan your work and work your plan. Surround yourself with a sound support system and hang out with like-minded people. Because "It ain't always easy, if it were, everybody would be doing it."

My Family Bond and Ties

As a family, we were not immune to significant, life-changing events. The most traumatic and impactful thus far was the loss of my eldest brother, Elton (henceforth to be referenced as "Tweety") in 2006, at the age of forty-seven. For context, as brothers, we were a formidable and cohesive reflection of the discipline, work ethic, love, and competitiveness that our parents had poured into us every day. To say we were inseparable and united souls might be an understatement. We were undeniably more affectionate than most siblings and even sisters.

Within the span of one year, Tweety was diagnosed with three life-threatening conditions. But he'd be quick to tell you, "It's really not that bad," "What's going on at the NCAA Track Meet?" "Did you hear that new song by…" I leveraged his approach and messaging when I found myself at crossroads in my life. If you met Tweety, you would remember him.

19

He would leave a warm impression of concern, confidence, humor, and optimism—more sprinklings of our DNA strains.

He gave selflessly to others without expectation or explanation. While here, Tweety brought so many incredible people into our lives before departing, so they would remain close to us, and subsequently, close to him. He was strategic. To get to my parent's house, you have to drive by his gravesite.

Tweety is often the topic of tales that will put a smile on your face and make you laugh to the point of pain. We celebrate him and the gifts he gave and left for us often. You know you've made the most of your life and created a legacy when people who never met you know exactly who you are fifteen years after your departure.

So as a family, we remained united around him until the end, and our bond is even stronger now as brothers. Not a month goes by without the three of us seeing each other, usually twice a month. While some siblings might look for excuses to be apart, we will create lame excuses to be together. When we are together, that three-legged stool seems to have an invisible but strong fourth leg. We are one because we know no other way.

We have been learning to live as three but are guided by the power of four. You never get over the loss of a loved one. But each day, we wake up and find a way to get through it. Every day is uncharted territory. The sadness and emptiness we feel in our hearts is the price of love. I've learned that memories and pain are precious eternal gifts that can be opened with or without notice. At 59, I know there is a minimal downside to this kind of love.

As adults, we've been asked on occasion, "Really, do you guys have to hug and kiss each other like that all the time?" Our response was, "Well yes, yes we do. So don't hate, replicate." Tomorrow is not promised to you. But one thing that you can be sure of is every day you rise; you are one day closer to your sunset. The day of departure for most of us is an unknown data point. So my advice? Forgive others and yourself quickly, let people who are important to you know that they are important to you, don't sweat the small stuff, stop and reflect periodically, be genuinely self-aware, and challenge yourself to grow and evolve into the best version imaginable.

More Family Celebrations and Reflections

Each year, family bonds are tested and subsequently strengthened. Sometimes it is based on joyous occasions such as new additions, graduations, marriages, and accomplishments, but we are even more united when illness, obstacles, or the loss of a family member occurs.

My 59th year has been no different. We celebrated the birth of Myles, Rhythm, and Keon Idris. We also celebrated Alex's college graduation, Bruce's executive promotion after successfully returning from the grips of COVID-19, and Brian's appointment to our alma maters advisory board. Additionally, we celebrated my father-in-law Leroy Jefferson's 90th birthday. Collectively, we somberly paid homage for the loss of my dear sweet cousin, Joni, and to the beautiful lives of two of my family's matriarchs, my aunt Veora and my mother-in-law, Mrs. Jefferson.

About my Mother-in-law

Elegance, grace, tenacity, faith, and love rolled into a beautiful, dark, timeless crystal is my mother-in-law, Jean Maudry Mills Jefferson. When you looked at her, especially up close, you knew she was different. Time, wisdom, perseverance, heartache, and strength had intricately honed her character.

She commanded respect by her presence, words, and actions. Without saying a word, you knew when she arrived and when she departed. By some accounts, Mrs. Jefferson was the original version of the E. F. Hutton commercial; "When she talked, people listened."

She taught me:

- <u>That a man in a suit should always have a handkerchief, not a hand towel.</u>
- To look people in the eye when you are serious about something.
- That, as a man, the bar is high, and people watch not just what you say, but what you do.
- That tough love should be delicately sprinkled on children and vigorously poured on adults.

She was full of whimsical wisdom, such as:

- You always knew when enough had been said: "Now looky here!"
- If she told you to "walk slow," it was not just sound advice; it was also a term of endearment.
- When asked how she was doing, depending on the day, she'd sometimes reply, "I may be kicking, but I'm not kicking high."
- If someone was trying to pull the wool over her eyes, she'd quickly let them know: "I might be an apple, but I ain't plum crazy!"
- After making her point, she'd seek verbal confirmation. She'd look you dead in your eye and say, "You hear what I'm saying to you (pause)…Right?"

Beautiful inside and out, that was this precious woman I had known and loved since 1983. She and my mom were united by our marriage, but became close friends by choice. The same is true for our fathers. In-laws that go out of their way to see each other? Now that's an atypical stereotype. Janel and I finally realized just how connected they were when we started traveling. I would tell my mom, "We're gonna go hiking in Sedona in a couple of weeks." My mother-in-law would inform Janel about it the next day. They laughed, prayed, gossiped, and strategized about Palm Sunday, Easter, Christmas, and Nativity displays.

When our parents traveled out to California to see us, it was funny, but not shocking, when our mothers arrived unknowingly wearing matching sweatshirts. Married for 71 years, Mr. and Mrs. Jefferson raised the bar high. I love my in-laws; they are my family.

COVID-19 provided another humbling reflection point for my family. Finally, after five months of self-imposed quarantine, my brothers and immediate family reunited. That may not seem like a long time, but when you are used to being together a minimum of two weekends a month, that's an eternity.

For the record, while I am relatively strong mentally, I am proudly "the weakest link" when it comes to my brothers. After uniting, I was sobbing uncontrollably; I inadvertently closely followed my brothers around the house. I was talking and keeping them in my sight. I didn't even realize I was doing it until I bumped into them a couple of times. That night, we brothers visited into the wee hours of the morning.

When it comes to taking care of our parents, we instinctively and efficiently triage each situation. We are a force to be reckoned with—a well-oiled machine with crisp communication and "just in time" outcomes—always delivered with the highest level of customer service, quality, and care.

Tony is in charge of external operations and food service delivery and makes sure the yard is immaculately maintained, military-style, like dad likes. Along with his partner in crime, Marilyn, they do all the grocery shopping and daily drive-bys. They are the primary point of contact, command central, and the "boots on ground" errand runners.

As our designated administrator, Brian is "on-call" and dispensed for public and religious speaking engagements on behalf of the family. Our spokesman and technical expert, he is responsible for keeping mom's devices operating. He never comes home without bringing something special for them to eat. He is our buffer, our secret weapon, frequently showing up unannounced but always right on time.

I am the General Manager (GM) of internal operations: primary chef, secondary errand runner, trash and maintenance supervisor, refrigerator organizer, light bulb changer, and overnight liaison. I make sure things run smoothly, or as they say, "I keep the lights on." As GM, my primary goal is to make sure our parents are constantly spoiled with an abundance of love, conversation, and food, just like they did for us. We do everything without hesitation, negotiation, confrontation, or a sense of obligation, or explanation, but instead out of unwavering respect, honor, and love.

My parents instilled a strong work ethic in us, not just through words but also by their actions. Growing up, we were reminded on many occasions to take pride in whatever task we performed, which included cutting the yard. As a Management Consultant specializing in Human Resources, I have leveraged these lessons throughout my career.

There is no more valuable asset to an organization than its people. Nothing happens without people, and great things only happen when you allow them to bring—and be—their "best self." There are no shortcuts to success, but the path is more transparent and logical when leaders lead by example.

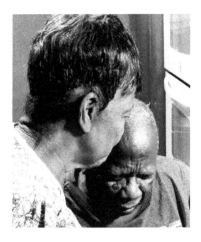

What leaders do is essential, but how they do it is even more important (consider critical). A wise leader understands the power of their words and actions and uses them with good intention.

If I had to pick one phrase or quote that best describes me and my outlook on life, it would have to be: "Treat people like you would want to be treated." I've been practicing this long before I was able to articulate it. I'm not sure why or how; it just seemed to be natural and the right thing to do. Fifty-nine years later, I still lead with this approach, and to date, the results have been overwhelmingly positive, with myself ultimately being the beneficiary. If you are a leader, be the kind of leader you want to work for, with, or follow. If you are unable to do so, then recuse yourself. You're a cog in the wheel.

When my kindness is not reciprocated, rather than try to convert someone or retaliate, I choose the quickest and most respectful departure route available. You never know what someone is going through. That day, that moment could be a terrible one for them. So rather than judge them or take it personally, I choose peace.

If my "something's not right" antenna goes up, I pause confidently but solemnly to see if their response changes. Sometimes a step back or standing still is progress.

I'm not an interventionist by nature, but believe a more targeted word might leave them in a better place. For the record, I have had several positive second re-encounters that validated my approach. Heck, if truth be told, it is possible to catch me on a bad day. We're all humans responding to the ebb and flow of life's currents. When you shine your light, it could remind others to turn on their own.

CHAPTER 2

MY PATH

"Everyone has their own path. Walk yours with integrity and wish all others peace on their journey."—Unknown

In the fall of 1980, I started college on a track scholarship—my primary goal was to obtain a degree in Finance. Things happened. Good things, the best thing in my life, happened. I met Janel Jefferson in the fall of 1981.

Just a little about Janel (a little because she consistently and intentionally flies under the radar): she epitomizes the phrase, "Actions speak louder than words." She is, without a doubt, the best gift God has given me. She is beautiful inside and out. I didn't just marry up, I married beyond. Beyond anything I dared, dreamed, or deserved.

We met in San Marcos, Texas, at Southwest Texas State University (aka Texas State University) in 1981. We started dating in 1983, were engaged in 1984, graduated in the Summer of 1986, and married December 6, 1986. She received her Bachelor of Fine Arts with a concentration in Studio Art. Together we became "The Artist" and "The Nerd."

Janel is an accomplished artist in her own right and an avid ancestral and historical researcher. Being featured in the Austin American-Statesman Newspaper, KUT-FM, and KLRU-TV (an Austin Public Broadcasting Station) is testimony to her talent. She has had two amazing solo gallery shows, and her art stately resides in many homes. Her work recreates prosperous African-Americans from post-reconstruction to the Harlem Renaissance, her use of color, texture, and form creating captivating and reflective portraits of past generations.

Janel paints portraits she would like to see on staircases in homes or wherever the homeowner appreciates them most. These are grand, formal, stately portraits of

African-Americans from generations past. Portraits in which people wear their best clothing, in which women wear elaborate hats adorned with flowers, and men wear straw boaters. Framed ornately, the paintings all measure at least 4 feet by 4 feet. Some are larger. In scale and commanding presence, they are reminiscent of the imperious portraits of royalty that line palace walls—or a formal picture of a long-ago family ancestor that hangs above a mantelpiece.

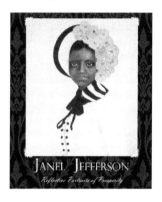

Her work currently resides in over 70 homes. If you are ever in Austin, swing by the "W" Hotel. One of her pieces, Marla, greets you in the main lobby, prominently displayed behind the registration desk. Walk down the halls of Dell's Children Hospital, and you will see the portrait of a brother and sister whose beautiful eyes seem to reach out to welcome you.

As a historical explorer and researcher, Janel was instrumental in having two African-American 100-plus-year-old community and religious structures recognized in Washington County, Texas, with official markers from the State of Texas Historical Commission. She is an active supporter and volunteer curator for the museum in Brenham, Texas. Some of the most popular exhibits have been for Juneteenth celebrations and World War I Black Veteran Shows. Janel uses her talent to highlight and speak for those no longer here and whose voices were marginalized. She also donates time and artwork to the artists' campaign to help immigrants and refugees, "Build Hope, Not Walls." The fruits of her labor will live on and be recognized for their excellence long after she is gone.

We have been together for 38 years (or 64.4% of my life). She is my life, and we are one. It is glaringly apparent to me that I am the real beneficiary. She knows me better than I know myself, and that's not just a cliché. When out for dinner and there are perplexing menu options, I ask without hesitation, "Honey, will I like that?" With a glance, she quickly sifts through the pros and cons related to my unsophisticated taste buds. She provides corroborating evidence before pronouncing an undeniable verdict, "Yes, you'll like it, and this is why..." She has seen me at what I believe to be my worst and declared it confidently, nothing more than a defining moment that she knew I could and would overcome. During each of my medical setbacks, it was Janel who pulled me through. Not allowing me to sulk or lament about my situation, she instead challenged me to get up and do something about it: focus on what I could control, and forget about the rest. When hospitalized at UCLA, weak and disoriented, she had my back and even used those blessed artist hands to bathe me.

I am a better, more open-minded, and humbler person because of her. I often tell people, "Before I met Janel, I thought crayons only came in eight colors. Now I know red is not always red. There's a sixty-four pack of crayons with seafoam, teal, magenta, fuchsia, and every other color known to humanity." She shines a bright and cheerful light on my thoughts, perspectives, and life.

She knows me better than anyone else and loves me

despite the proprietary historical knowledge she possesses of many of my shortcomings. More than ninety-five percent of the time, she is right. From time to time, when I finally realize it, with a smile, she'll matter of factly say, "Of course I'm right, that's why I'm the wife."

We have weathered many storms during life's journey and experienced all of our marriage vows: richer or poorer, better or worse, sickness and health. We have supported, encouraged, and loved one another uniquely since our first date thirty-eight years ago. There is but one marital vow left for us to experience, **until death do us part**.

Our 25th wedding anniversary celebration was planned to reunite the many people who have brightened our lives over the years. There was no exchanging of rings, renewal of wedding vows, or declarations of love. Everyone there knew us,

and over the past 25 years, our actions have spoken louder than any nuptial traditions. It was time to reunite, listen to music, eat, and have a party! Here are a few of those special moments and people from December 3, 2011. We are blessed.

Life has a way of inserting a little equilibrium into our experiences—mixing challenging and precious moments to test our resilience, provide a few rays of hope, and re-enforce those really significant things. Here's one of many unanticipated priceless memories:

DAD: (After arriving from his Monday dialysis treatment) "Son, Do you think we can swing by Sweet Home Cemetery so I can see my mom and dad?"

ME: (While simultaneously canceling and rescheduling all of today's remaining meetings within two minutes!) "Dad, absolutely; I'd love to see them too. It's been way too long. Give me five more minutes, and I'll pull the car around front."

REWARD: New and precious data uploaded to my "cloud." During the picturesque and quiet hillside drive (no radio), I carefully listened to him talk about when, where, and how he picked cotton. I was shocked to hear he walked nine miles (one-way) into town regularly. I was literally a sponge, soaking in all the invaluable wisdom being poured into me. NOTE: I purposely drove well below every posted speed limit, trying to milk the moment.

CONCLUSION: Those two hours were far more productive, life-changing, engaging, and educational than ANY weeklong executive strategic planning retreat I have ever attended. The circle of life often closes far too soon on so many of our loved ones. It is a fact—hundreds of reliable sources have validated that, myself included. My summation: "Leave no deed, thought, word or emotion on the opposite end of the table when it comes to your parents."

If you still have the opportunity, make sure that they are, without a doubt, the absolute priority. Fortunately, I am blessed to have both of my parents, and I don't need any testimonials to encourage me to value them and act accordingly. I have seen and solemnly supported so many dear friends and family members during their parents' transitions, each time fully realizing that I am just another day, step, and second closer to being in their place.

Suppose your parents, or your elders for those that matter, make what you quickly classify as a non-urgent request. Please try to understand it from their perspective. For them, the clock is ticking a lot louder than it used to. Please remember, their event horizon is a lot closer than yours.

FOOD & MUSIC

After family, my biggest vices are food, travel, and music. Although I consider myself an introvert, there's a common denominator amongst these activities—people. So maybe I'm just borderline introverted. Personally and professionally, I believe that strong relationships are crucial to growth and happiness.

Anyone who knows me knows that I love all things food, not only for what it is and how it makes you feel but for what it does. It brings people together. It is an integral part of my family's connectivity. Many people have put their feet under my parent's kitchen table and later struggled to get up. During your stay, you would be doused with love and hugs. We celebrated their 60th wedding anniversary in epic style by preparing a Texas-style BBQ brunch as a send-off to the attendees. We (brothers and cousins) blocked off the street, pulled in five pits, and grilled. When the smoke settled, we prepared 38 ribs, 24 dozen chicken wings, 70 pounds of sausage, and 20 whole chickens.

I have three partners in crime, my BBQ pits: Martha, Fletcher, and R2D2. Martha is the queen, bequeathed to me by my dad in 1996. Martha has traveled with me to California and back. Together, we have filled the stomachs of several neighborhood friends, family, and a few strangers. In 2020, I fired up my pits a total of twenty-six times, an average of once every other week. Don't get me wrong, I love to eat, but most of what I cook I share with others. To me, the process of transforming something generic into something unique is rewarding and therapeutic. Given that 2020 was a challenging year globally with COVID-19, there probably was no safer and peaceful place to be than in my backyard hanging out with Martha and Fletcher.

Don't threaten me with a good time! I get excited when neighbors bring more product. I'll take it, season it, grill it, package it, and then text them when it's ready. "Your package is ready on fence post four!" The smoke is exquisite and is a natural conversation starter. I have met dozens of people over the fence. This year, after a five-month hiatus (more about that in **My Journey**), I fired up Martha. Two hours into the cook, I got a text from a neighbor three blocks away but downwind. "I can smell Martha! What are you grilling?"

My dad, and by some measures his brothers, are responsible for guiding me down this culinary path. Food was an integral part of our family gatherings while growing up. Food drew us together not just to enjoy incredible meals seasoned with love but to reflect on our blessings and strengthen our bonds. After years of grueling apprenticeship, in 1996, I received his Phase IV Pitmaster certificate, which is framed and proudly displayed in my home office.

In the Spring of 2020, I created a Facebook Food Page called *EpicuriousThe1*. There reside 1000+ photos, my secret recipes, famous and not-so-famous but skilled culinary professionals, great places to eat, and annual BBQ events. In addition, there are dozens of Live videos of me "in action," honing the craft. Oh, did I mention I have a spreadsheet called Michael's Central Texas BBQ Reconnaissance? I created it after 12 years in southern California. We returned home to Austin in 2014, and I was able to take a year-long sabbatical. I was spending the majority of that time recharging my professional batteries by unplugging from all things business. One of my goals was to make up for lost time by sampling good old Texas BBQ. There are so many delicious establishments; I prefer the small town or non-commercialized joints. To me, if you have more than three locations, you're not a BBQ joint, and in extreme cases, you're fringing on being a fast-food BBQ place. I shy away from those.

I prefer well-cured buildings that serve meals on butcher paper, with no frills, friendly staff, and consistent product. The kind of place where you leave, and a couple of hours later, you've got that smoke cologne in your clothes. So far, I've been to 34 different BBQ joints within a 100-mile radius of Austin. I meticulously rate them holistically by the ambiance, price, consistency, and major offerings. I include notes as a reminder of why I didn't like the brisket or who makes the best sausage blend. My Top Five has remained so since I started. I guard my spreadsheet to protect the names of the bottom dwellers. I respect anyone who pursues that career; it's a lot of hard work, long hours, and dedication, so there is no need to bash anyone publicly. I know where to go and where not to go. I will gladly take you places you have never been before. Don't threaten me with a good time! Even now, there are still twenty-two places "in the queue." Eating BBQ is hard work, but someone's got to do it. Fortunately, I'm not alone. My brother Brian and my cousin John have the same issues.

Moving right along! Music does make the world go round. So I've been doing my part to help keep it spinning. Like good food, music also has a way of bringing people together. I love all kinds of music and always have six CDs loaded in my car and twelve in the glove compartment. Yes, I still have a CD player. I love the flexibility to create my versions of "The Best of" or "genre compilations." I currently have seventy-three different playlists, and if I had the time, it would take approximately 36.4 days non-stop to listen to the entire collection. I've shared thousands of CDs with family, friends, and anyone who's asked or expressed an interest in music. Most of them arrive in the mail unannounced and are often targeted to help someone meet a challenging moment in their life—my way of saying, "You good?" These random acts of kindness require minimal time, effort, or inconvenience.

Throughout my journey, I relied heavily on faith and music for solace and resolve. Adele, The Bee Gees, Bonnie Raitt, David Bowie, The Brothers Johnson, Bliss, Camiel, The Commodores, Con Funk Shun, The Doobie Brothers, **Earth, Wind & Fire**, Elton John, Fat Jon, Roberta Flack, Funky

DL, Marvin Gaye, HER, Heatwave, The Jackson's, Journey, K. D. Lang, Maxwell, Curtis Mayfield, Pat Metheny, George Michael, Midnight Star, Mint Condition, Nujabes, Prince, Reki, Seal, Sting, James Taylor, Tears For Fears, Thievery Corporation, Toto, Luther Vandross, and War were a few of my lyrical companions.

If I had to pick an anthem for 2021, it would be *Better Days* by Ant Clemons and Justin Timberlake. I listened to it religiously. The words were inspiring and relevant during **My Journey**.

CAREER TRANSITIONS & SUPPORT

To me, work is what I do, but it is not who I am. Don't get me wrong; I was taught at an early age, "You either do something, or you don't; there's no middle ground." Always strive to be the best, whatever it is you pursue. I have found that most of my attributes have professional application. When I tap into them, I can triangulate complex or tense work situations through a different lens. Just keep in mind that 99.9% of the time, despite the sense of urgency, magnitude of the crisis, or pressure to deliver, there are usually no life-threatening implications to what you are sincerely trying to achieve. Pause, taking a minute to gather yourself, especially if you are in a leadership role. Others will be looking to you for guidance and at you for your demeanor and body language. Choose your words carefully; they can become a part of your legacy. If/when you find yourself facing a tough business decision with potential implications to others, ask yourself, "How would I want to be treated or feel if I was sitting on the other side of the table or the receiving end of this message?" Then if needed, adjust your approach, communication, and mindset accordingly.

After 25 years in the corporate world, I began to feel the wear and tear. So it was time to transition to the next phase of my professional life as a Management Consultant. I realized that I could probably add more value working with organizations than working for them. I subsequently built my own Human Resource consulting business around this simple but strategic, straightforward approach: challenging business decisions become less complex and stressful if/when you put people first.

Unfortunately, during my career, I have directly or indirectly played a role in the termination of hundreds of people. It's not something I wear as a badge of honor but something I approached as a sacred responsibility. Most of the layoffs were due to corporate restructuring and were based on non-performance-related business decisions. However, that does not make the communication or process less intense or stressful for the impacted individuals. These are life- and career-changing conversations. I prepare myself for the economics of the discussion and gather as much professional and personal information on the affected individual. I have been involved in termination discussions and initiatives that have impacted close colleagues, friends, and family members. I often say, "It's not the what, but the how," that gives you the courage and compassion to do your job with humanity.

These are when the words "treat people like you would want to be treated" become actionable. That conversation is the last discussion retained by the departing staff. While they may not always understand why they were terminated, they will never forget how they were treated. There is no substitute for respect, integrity, compassion, and transparency. If done well, when it's over, you'll be able to look yourself in the eye.

Now, I am in the fortunate position to leverage my experience and talent:

1. I do only what I enjoy doing, not what someone else tells me to do.
2. I dictate the hours that I work.
3. I determine the value of my work.
4. I no longer have to play the game and am not concerned about being on a succession planning chart or preparing for a management performance review.
5. I don't deal with red tape, politics, or having to justify my time off.
6. Most importantly, I decide exactly to whom I will and who I will not provide my professional services.

After making the move, I realized that I was actually at the top of my game but playing for the wrong team. Personally or professionally, if you don't like something, you have to do something about it. Complaining and complacency are not your friends and will succeed at making you bitter. Bitterness is a virus that can infect several critical pillars in your life, causing them and your spirit to spiral out of control.

Take a second and think about the five things that you'll miss most when your final sun is setting. Suppose you're willing and able to prioritize them. Think about where and how you are spending your time and energy today. How much of it is being spent on your Top Five (T5)? If it's important enough to be one of the things you'll miss most, it should be significant enough to consume a big portion of your time, right? Your T5 should align with and reflect where you are in your life's journey. There is no right or wrong list. Remember, things change, we change, and life changes. So every five to ten years, your T5 needs recalibration. The goal is to make sure your time allocation continues to give you the best return on investment based on your event horizon. T5 priorities can move up, down, or drop off to make room for new ones.

My T5: family, friends, impact, peace, and sharing my life experiences. The last two are new additions within the last two years.

In times of doubt, don't forget about the things you've had to overcome to get to this point in your life. Give yourself some credit because there will be times when no one else will. If you are confronting adversity with limited life resources to draw from, draw from the experiences of others, including myself. But first, make sure the challenge really exists and is not just in your mind. At times, we can be our worst enemy. We're human, and sometimes we create or dwell on situations that have yet to be or may never manifest themselves. Time offers no refunds on misspent energy. Try to understand what you can control and develop a mindset that waits to worry. More than 99% of the time, you will survive. It's essential to think about how you want to feel and be seen by others when you come out on the other side. You will most likely emerge from the dark clouds. This is your moment to inspire others. Don't underestimate the power of optimism and faith.

CHAPTER 3

MY TRAVELS

"We travel not to escape life, but for life not to escape us."
– Unknown

We have traveled together to every continent except for Australia and Antarctica. It all started with a trip to Fairbanks, Alaska, to visit family. Along the way, we took a detour and stayed at Denali National Park and Reserve. Next, we struck out on a seven-mile hike on Mount Healy Overlook Trail. With each step, we became more intrigued and in awe of nature. We loved the compelling effort versus reward proposition and vowed to seek out more of these challenges. From there, it developed into a passion for trekking, going off the beaten path, pushing ourselves physically and mentally, and experiencing those unique things that make the world a majestic and beautiful place. With each adventure, we learned more about ourselves and others.

Some of our international adventures include Mexico City, Amsterdam, Mount Kilimanjaro (Tanzania), Lima (Peru), Santiago (Chile), Melaque Bay, Jalisco (Mexico), Kathmandu (Nepal), the cradle of humanity at Ngorongoro Crater (Tanzania); Ambergris Caye (Belize), the Mayan ruins at Chichen Itza (Mexico) the mystical moai at Easter Island, Machu Picchu (Peru), Toronto (Canada), trekking to Kala Pattar in the Himalaya's (Nepal), Bangkok (Thailand) and hiking the "W" in Patagonia (Chile). Our lives were enriched by these places, cultures, and the people who welcomed us at every destination. Yet, there is still so much that remains on our bucket list. We intend to make the most of our time here together.

We have met and become close friends with people we would not have met otherwise during our travels. We also realized just how blessed we've been. Things we take for granted, like running water, flushing toilets, drinkable water, electricity, transportation, opportunity, etc., are not automatically available. At each destination, we were warmly greeted and fortunate to experience nothing but kindness, encouragement, pride, and gratitude through our travels. For most of our adventures, Janel was the photographer, and I was the journalist. Occasionally, we reminisce by enjoying the photos and gifts from our travels.

In life, whenever the opportunity presents itself, strive to leave people in a better place, position, or state of mind than where they were before you met. Someday, someone might do the same for you.

May 1999, Machu Picchu on the Inca Trail – Our entourage consisted of eight porters, one cook, and a guide (Adriel). On the last morning, our porters were pretty excited; the tour company paid them $5 per day, and this day was payday ($20 apiece). We tipped them an additional $40 each and gave them two sacks full of power bars, tea, candy, and nuts.

One thing I took away from this trip was a deep respect for porters. Our porters were between 18-24 years old. They'd set up camp and take care of all the details, singing songs in Quechua. We would leave them each morning, setting out on the trail while they packed up our belongings. Without fail, they would pass us within an hour. While we struggled along the trail, they would jog by us, fully burdened with supplies. It was a humbling experience.

October 2000, Kilimanjaro and Ngorongoro Crater, Tanzania – The Chagga are Tanzania's third-largest group and live on the slopes of Kilimanjaro. Cultivating the mountainside, they are noted for their enterprise and hard work. They developed irrigation systems to carry water up to 600 feet above the river level, enabling them to sustain the plants from which they brew beer.

Our porters ranged from 18-27 years old. They climbed these rugged mountain peaks one or two times a month, using the money as a means to support small farms and purchase necessities. During our time on the mountain, they treated us with the utmost respect and kindness, and we took every opportunity to let them know they were the best part of our Africa experience. We thanked them for sharing their country, customs, and the mountain with us.

We remembered most of them by name: God's Love, Desmas, Stehan, Paul, and Joachim, the lead guide. Sadly, we knew this would be the last time that we would probably ever see them again. We gave them our ski pants, thermal socks, gloves, thermal shirts, long johns, and power bars.

We thanked them for taking us on the most challenging journey of our lives and bringing us back down in one piece. The celebration was capped off with the porters singing a Swahili tribute to hikers returning from the mountain. Their voices, harmony, and words were absolutely beautiful.

Dominating northern Tanzania and the area known as the Massai Steppe, these tall, proud people are easily recognizable by their single toga-like piece of clothing (called shukas) – usually bright red or blue. One thing we quickly realized is that no matter where you go, children are children. These kids laughed, joked, cried, and squabbled just like kids anywhere else on earth. We had brought some colored pens and other supplies for them. (Insert 6.6 – Children)

We spent our last night in Africa in a luxury hotel located on the rim of the Ngorongoro Crater. After enjoying an incredible dinner, we hung around for a bit. Our hosts were gracious, and we wanted to spend some time with them. After all the diners left, we were rewarded with an emotional and bonding night with the staff. Before it was over, we felt as if we were hanging out with old friends. Based on my DNA origins and my roots, perhaps we were. They were glad that we took the time to learn their language, history, and culture. We were happy they welcomed us with open arms. As the night wound down, there would be lots of heartfelt hugs and goodbyes.

One of our most incredible memories from our travels occurred on Mt. Kilimanjaro, on the Machame Trail. On the fifth night on the mountain, we camped on the sloping ridge at 12,600 feet (or 3,840 meters) at the Shira Plateau. To the west, we could see the caldera and rim of Mount Meru, the fifth highest peak in Africa (14,845 ft or 4526 m). As the sun set and the temperatures dropped, an incredible ocean-like fog ascended up the ridge against a moonlit backdrop. The air was light, crisp, and clear. We knew this was a precious, once-in-a-lifetime experience. So we took it all in until darkness filled the night sky, and the temperatures rapidly dropped into the single digits. And here I am some 20 years later reflecting on that evening on the mountain.

The world is big but gets much smaller if/when you take the time to engage with people. Different experiences shape us, but we are all anchored in humanity. While our religions, politics, and economic situations might differ, our individual needs and aspirations are similar. Relationships don't have to be complicated. Unfortunately, we create artificial barriers that limit opportunities to learn, grow, and evolve.

I have had the privilege of meeting so many incredible people in this great big old world. Quite a few I consider friends, and a subset I consider close friends. For the record, I constantly filter access and judiciously manage my inner circle, in the end allowing only a tiny percentage of those relationships to occupy space on my social terra firma ultimately. This is a real-life example of "less is more" and "quality is more important than quantity."

I am truly blessed to have remained in close contact with and continue to be a part of many individuals' lives on every continent except Australia and Antarctica. I am, without a doubt, a much better version of myself after being exposed to different cultures, people, perspectives, and realities. Travel assuredly enriches the heart, mind, and soul of the adventurer.

Glacier cruise patagonia chile

We are not through with our travel adventures. After taking a brief pause to face life events, we have plans. We have set our sights on an around-the-world trip: twenty-four days and eleven destinations on six continents. Our first stop will be Cusco, Machu Picchu, and the North Coast or Peru, then back to Easter Island, Chile, on to Nadi, Fiji, the Great Barrier Reef, Australia, Angkor Wat, Cambodia, Taj Mahal and Jaipur, India, Serengeti Plains and returning to Ngorongoro Crater, Tanzania, then on to the Luxor and Cairo, Egypt, Petra, Jordan and finally Marrakech, Morocco. Stay tuned!

CHAPTER 4

MY HEADWINDS

*"Our very survival depends on our
ability to stay awake, to adjust to new ideas,
to remain vigilant, and to face the challenge of change."*
—*Martin Luther King Jr.*

In life, no one gets out unscathed. At some point, we all experience some of the negative things that life offers. Not every day or everyone can be sunny and bright. Dark clouds are up there too. I've always said, "It's not what happens to you, it's how you choose to respond." But as I have learned, sometimes adhering to the advice I provide others can be difficult.

My parents prepared us well for most of life's challenges. A lot of potential can be preempted by treating people the way you would want to be treated. However, that approach doesn't work when you encounter racism, prejudice and hatred. The moral compass of its possessor is irreparably skewed, calibrated by centuries-old views, false stereotypes, insecurity, money, and the desire to maintain power and control. These positions cannot be generalized across a particular race or ethnicity. They are individual choices.

Of all the headwinds I have faced in my 59 years, this one has brought tears, anger, fear, and disbelief. What follows are real-life examples of the "normal" that has shaped the lives of myself and many others. We are more resilient, but less optimistic, because we understand that there is no end to suffering in our lifetime.

At times, I'll admit that, given my optimistic approach and outlook on life, I am often perplexed when race immediately supersedes character. In terms of evaluation criteria, this lens is the polar opposite of how I was raised and what I believe, which is to see and treat people based on who they are and how they treat others but never based on what they look like. I have walked a straight line during my life, so to experience unwarranted and blatant scrutiny has taken a toll on me.

I understand why some athletes use their platforms to highlight racial injustice. There is nothing American about racism other than it has survived for more than four centuries. Ask yourself, "Would I be motivated and proud to stand up for something that remains aspirational for me, despite generations of sacrifice and loyalty by my family?" If your answer is yes, then I respectfully ask that you look up the definition of integrity. A flag is symbolic and devoid of life. I place more value on life and our actions than materialistic objects, but that's just me.

The facts are what they are. The data does not lie. African-Americans are 60 percent more likely to be stopped by police even though, as a whole, they drive 16 percent less. When taking into account less time on the road, blacks are about 95 percent more likely to be stopped. We are 110 percent more likely than our Caucasian brethren to be searched in a traffic stop (5.0 percent for blacks, 2.4 percent for our counterparts). In the end, contraband was more likely to be found in searches of non-black drivers.

Simply stated, we are stopped more on the pretext of having done something wrong. Upon not finding what they thought they might find, which remains a mystery, we are permitted to go on our way, more often than not, without apology or explanation. Over time, that will make you a little paranoid and a lot more defensive and bitter. It places an asterisk in your mind while saying the last three words of the Pledge of Allegiance, "justice for all." We still say them, but like our centuries-old gospel hymns, there's a lot of pain, hurt and open wounds in doing so. For some, those three words remain aspirational. I believe that:

- Exchanging wedding rings does not make someone faithful.
- Wearing a cross does not make someone religious.
- Saluting a flag does not make someone a patriot.
- Saying a pledge (to a flag) does not make someone honor it.

I've always placed more value on actions versus symbolism. One is tangible and reveals a person's character, the other an inanimate representation of a lofty future state.

But that's just my opinion, and one of the components of my moral compass. I don't feel the need to debate it or persuade anyone to agree at all. Different experiences can provide a different lens to view the world. To each their own.

Driving Without Benefits (aka Driving While Black or DWB)

Police Officer (PO): "Nice car, is it yours?"

Driver: *He thinks I stole this car. Just answer without any emotion or facial expressions.* "Officer, is there a problem? Did I do something wrong?"

PO: (After ignoring the Driver's question) "Can I see your driver's license, registration, and insurance?"

Driver: *Ok, Cool. Let him know it's in the glove compartment before reaching over to open it.*

PO: "Do you have any drugs in the car?" Driver: *He thinks I use drugs. Just calmly answer the question.* "No sir, I do not."

PO: "Do you sell any drugs?"

Driver: *He thinks I'm a drug dealer. Deep breath. Stay calm; just answer the question.* "No sir, I do not."

PO: "Do you have any firearms?" Driver: *Keep your hands on the steering wheel, just answer the question.* "No sir, I do not."

PO: "Do you have any large sums of money?

Driver: *He thinks I'm a drug dealer. Deep breath. Stay calm, just answer the question.* "No sir, I do not."

PO: "Are you a professional athlete?"

Driver: *Are you #^@! kidding me! Just answer the question, I guess I'm not supposed to own or be driving a nice car unless I'm a drug user, dealer, or professional athlete.* "No sir, I am not. I am a Human Resource and Management Executive."

The police officer taps the documents on the driver's window, then hands them back to the driver. He takes one more quick look at the passenger side, at the side door storage compartment, and down at the floor; then, peering skeptically into the back seat, he nods and backs away.

PO: "OK, you're good to go. Be careful out here." The driver did not respond or make eye contact this time but stared as if in a trance, looking straight ahead through the front windshield. Stoic.

FACT: This is what happened to me in Texas in 2015, after being pulled over for no apparent reason. Afterward, I was shaking; my heart was racing and I was emotionally upset. Clutching the steering wheel, with tears welling up in my eyes, I asked myself, "Are you kidding me? You just can't win; sooner or later, this is not going to end well for me." Funny that I have to think about this in terms of being lucky. I'm a good person; this is just flat-out crazy! I spent the next 10 minutes sitting there on the side of the road wondering what to do next, unknowingly asking myself, *How can I stop this from keeping happening? I can't call Janel right now; I'm too upset; I just have to calm down; I know I'd start crying as soon as I heard her voice. What did I do to deserve this?*

Discrimination has evolved with time. The undertones are more covert now, but the reality is that it's no different than being on a plantation and being asked by the slave master, "Where are you going, boy?" It's systemic, modern-day racism, a way to keep a little tension in the chain. Unfortunately, racism is just as American as baseball and apple pie, only it's been around longer.

Given my physical appearance and the fact that I was driving a Lexus, I knew I had to do as my ancestors did— stay in my place. I didn't want to come across as bitter, hiding something, or give any reason for further interrogation or escalation. I'm just grateful that I was not harmed, tased, or locked up, and remained alive. I know that I'm not alone.

In a third such incident, Janel was with me, and we were questioned for having a bag of paperclips in the back seat. I was asked to get out of the car. For those who doubt its existence, I just wanted to get my story on the record, in case it happens again with a different outcome and there's no video to support my past responses and behavior.

So each day, I continue to follow several unspoken but necessary protocols to stay safe and ultimately alive. While many terrible things have happened, our nation is, fortunately, finally starting to see some small changes for the better. However, it looks like some things will never change, or if so, definitely not in my lifetime.

Departure Ritual

To survive, we evolve, developing new traditions, habits, and behaviors based on our real-life experiences, compassion for our loved ones, and out of pure necessity. I call this one my "departure ritual," which my mom and I instinctively perform whenever leaving their house. It goes something like this:

I give her a big hug and kiss before walking out to my car.
I sit down, close the door and pause, take a deep breath,
and sigh.
She stands nervously in the front doorway.
I roll the window down quickly.
I look over, smile, and say, "I love you mom." I remind her
that I'll call her first thing when I get home.
I slowly roll the window up and
I can see her mouthing the words, "Jesus, please cover
him."
She doesn't go into the house until I'm well down the
road.
I imagine what thoughts must be running through her
head.
Hopefully, they are not the same ones in mine.
I make a selection from one of the six pre-loaded CDs.

The departure ritual standard is my Gospel CD because I
know Mom's probably humming one now. It's another way
for me to stay grounded, optimistic and to keep us connected
spiritually.

For the record: Mom called me twice during the hour-
long, 60-mile drive home.

"Hey baby, I'm just checking in on you." "Hey baby, I'm
just checking in on you."

Performed as if permanently programmed to autoplay,
this biological maternal "departure ritual" happens at least
twenty to thirty times a year. It's just something required to
give us a glimmer of hope and, potentially, one last moth-
er-son bonding moment. We've done this dance ever since I
received my driver's license forty-one years ago. It's required,
but deprives us of what should be a peaceful drive home from

a precious family visit. This has been the norm for me and many others that just happen to "fit the profile."

WWB (Walking While Black)

Occasionally, I choose to venture a little further out of the neighborhood to change scenery and get some extra miles. A few safety tips need to be followed because of who I am and how I might be perceived. Here's an excerpt I journaled on what was going through my head during an extended neighborhood outing last year:

From an awareness perspective, my senses were on medium alert. I had my headphones on, so my head was on a swivel, gazing around periodically, but not too much so as not to look suspicious.

I wore my high visibility workout outfit and carried matching Gatorade (Orange top, black shorts, orange and black running shoes). No stealthy or covert-looking attire.

I made sure to casually transition from the sidewalk and quickly onto the street when the sidewalks got too close to any houses. Especially if there were a lot of protruding bushes, or the front yard was small. I gracefully maneuvered to the other side of the street when encountering oncoming walking traffic, especially women. I could see the relief on a few faces, but others waved, so I smiled.

I didn't stop to smell any roses or admire any houses. I took a quick glance and made some mental notes. "Man, that's some crazy architecture!" "I gotta show Janel that fence!"

Most importantly, I made sure I got my butt home before it got dark, even if it meant finishing strong with a little more recovery time.

For the record, I did pass four houses with *Black Lives Matter* signs in their front yard. I slowed down but did not stop to appreciate those houses. When I got home, I had logged five miles, but in the end, I'm not sure how much stress was released. Sigh.

More DWB Chronicles

I know a man—a proud, hardworking, God-fearing family man, married for less than ten years—who was driving with his wife, young daughter, and son attempting to get home after a tornadic event. After detouring around a car that police had pulled over, the officer abruptly turned around, lunged over and kicked his tire, and said, "Boy, didn't I tell you to pull over?"

The officer then approached and continued with this derogatory line of interrogation. The man repeatedly responded, "Sir, I'm just trying to get my family home." The officer responded at least two more times, beginning with the term "Boy," at which point, the man said, "Sir, you got one more time to call me 'boy' in front of my family." The wife quickly covered her husband's mouth, and thankfully the situation de-escalated.

The wife knew that a wrong answer to any officer's questions could result in her husband being tased, handcuffed, jailed, or killed. But the man knew that letting the officer demean him in front of his children would reinforce the reach of systemic bigotry and racism into the next generation. He was willing to put his life on the line to prevent that from happening.

That man was my brother.

Inevitably, I know I will get pulled over again. I know I fit that fictitious racial profile. However, I will approach the situation with the caution and respect it deserves. That's how I was raised, and besides, I know the potential consequences. I must tamper my ego and resentment and have faith in a positive outcome for the sake of those who love and need me.

I understand that the outcome depends entirely on the character of the individual that pulls me over. That's the moment where the rubber meets the road. When you're driving while black in rural Texas, it is the luck of the draw. There is absolutely nothing I can do about that except pray again for tangible change in my lifetime, not just ongoing systemic acceptance.

Just so we are clear, my struggle and wish is not retaliatory; my ultimate goal is to remain unharmed and stay alive. I am by nature a docile, caring, and non-aggressive person, a gentle giant. I believe all of my friends will attest to this fact. I just firmly believe color should not determine someone's character. We are our choices. Everyone should be judged on how they treat people and their individual choices and actions. Unfortunately, those are not universally held beliefs.

And just because you haven't experienced something doesn't mean it does not exist. And yes, just because it doesn't directly impact you, it is still wrong. Racism, hate, and discrimination are some of my least favorite words. Webster defines empathy as the ability to understand and share the feelings of another. We need more empathy today, even if it causes comfortability or results in seeing a reflection in the mirror. If you really care about someone going through this and have not spoken out loud or used your platform, your silence—intentional or not—is a subtle form of acceptance.

If the shoe were on the other foot, and you and I were friends, you'd know that I would speak up vocally and without hesitation. It's called integrity. Right or wrong does not have a color, neither does hate. Empathy and compassion are real things. I wish that those who do not believe or understand could walk in my shoes. You would stumble in disbelief with every fifth step taken.

At times, I was perplexed by the response (or lack thereof) of a few friends. Some I have known for most of my life. It was as if they knew racism existed, but it was something that we should all be used to and accept by now. It wasn't until I began to share my close encounters that it put a familiar face on this reality. Some reached out immediately to thank me for opening their eyes. They knew my life is based on equality, kindness, and inclusivity.

There have been a few moments of hope. So it is only fair that I share one of those moments and end this chapter with positivity. Unfortunately, even this recollection highlights some PTSD symptoms from growing up black.

I was waiting at the counter of a not to be named, but probably really familiar coffee shop for my Grande Non-Fat Mocha. A police officer came over behind me and said, "Sir, can I talk to you for a quick second?" Of course, I was thinking, *Ooookay, here we go....* I slowly stepped towards him with my hands by my side while quickly checking my internal list of the potential real or fictitious violations that might be coming my way. Then he quickly smiled and said, "Do you have an open carry permit for those guns (talking about my arms)?" We both busted out laughing! I pray for more of these types of close encounters.

These experiences are a sobering but critical part of my journey and played a pivotal role in becoming the person I am today. Without a doubt, omitting them would make *59 Prime* incomplete and diminish its intended value and purpose.

All that I and a growing rainbow of color minority human beings want are for these clouds of racism, hatred, and inequality to disappear. I would love not to talk about it.

I would love to experience what it feels like not to be treated and looked at differently. It sounds like a simple request, but power is an intoxicating and addictive elixir. I just hope that after 400 years, we're more than halfway to solving this worldwide problem. We can do better than this in America and abroad. Speak up, speak out. Your voice and conviction will undoubtedly carry more weight than mine/ours.

CHAPTER 5

MY JOURNEY

*"Your journey is not the same as mine, and my journey
is not yours. But if you meet me in a certain path,
may we encourage each other."—Unknown*

In 2002, life was really good in Austin, Texas. I worked for Dell Technologies, and my career path and progression were on the fast track. Then that spring, I was approached by a trusted former colleague and mentor about a potential opportunity with a small but growing and well-respected biotechnology company in Thousand Oaks, California, called Amgen. After researching the company and subsequently spending a fact-finding week to fully assess the company, people, culture, and financial implications, Janel and I decided this could be our "once in a lifetime" opportunity. It would mean leaving both of our close-knit families, but something about the timing, the company, and the opportunity felt right. After the decision was made, things quickly and conveniently started to fall into place as if this move had already been scripted. Our Austin home sold in two weeks, and we found and bought our new home in Simi Valley, California, within two months. Little did we know the significance of this move and how it would ultimately play a role in saving my life six years after our arrival. When I signed the offer letter, I didn't know it, but someone was watching over me, and this move was not a chance event. Had I accepted an employment offer elsewhere or decided to stay put in Texas, there is a high probability that *59 Prime* would never be written, at least not with my pen and from my lens.

Hospitalization: Round One

Fast forward to the spring of 2008. I almost passed out after coming back from working out at the company gym. My vision had become blurred, and my physical dexterity and cognitive ability were slightly impaired. I got off the elevator on the third floor and staggered directly down the hall and into my office. Spinning around as I dropped into my chair, I began sweating profusely and could barely hold my head up. I realized that I couldn't remember Janel's phone number. Finally, on the third attempt, I hit the preset number for my boss, Ted Bagley. Ted's office was on the fourth floor in the building adjacent to mine. He picked up, I mumbled a few words, and that's all I can remember, even now.

One of the infrequently discussed perks of being employed by an incredible, people-focused biotechnology company is having hundreds of doctors as colleagues scattered across the large headquarters. Within three minutes, urgent talking and activity were happening all around me. People came from every nook and cranny and converged into my small office. I tried to respond to the questions as I was being diagnosed. Then I quickly realized that I was on a gurney being rushed by ambulance to a nearby hospital for further testing and observation. Janel and Ted were there, and I awoke the next day back at home after a battery of tests. Something was amiss, but they couldn't pinpoint the exact cause or source but knew it impacted my sight and equilibrium.

Later that week, I had an appointment with my ophthalmologist. Something was putting an excessive amount of pressure on my optical nerves. After reviewing MRI and CAT scans and completing a visual dexterity test, he paused. The look on his face and his demeanor were telling. He abruptly left the room, then just as quickly returned. He had made a call to a colleague to share my results and discuss the next steps. "Michael, ummmm, I just scheduled an appointment for you to see a specialist this Friday." Well, it was more than just a specialist; it was the chief Neurosurgeon at Ronald Reagan UCLA Medical Center.

Three days later on Friday, we made the 45-minute drive into Los Angeles, cautiously optimistic, but I knew a meeting with the chief Neurosurgeon was not normal. After another MRI, blood work, and consultation with a Rheumatologist, it was determined that the excessive cranial inflammation—most likely bacterial or fluid—was placing pressuring my optical nerves. A biopsy would be needed to diagnose the root cause. So, an emergency craniotomy was scheduled for the following Monday.

A craniotomy is the surgical removal of part of the bone from the skull to expose the brain. Specialized tools are used to remove the section of the bone, called the bone flap. Depending on the patient's circumstances, the bone flap can be removed temporarily and replaced after surgery or, as in my case, removed and not replaced, but covered with a dura mesh patch, an organic implant base on equine collagen. Leaving my skull open would allow the swelling in my brain to subside post-surgery and make it accessible if future cranial treatment was required.

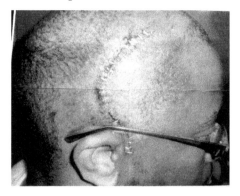

Initially, I didn't understand the sense of urgency to perform the procedure, but over the weekend, I would quickly realize just how ominous the situation had become. That Friday night, after returning from UCLA, I began to experience more loss of mobility and coordination. By Saturday evening, I began to experience double vision and extreme light sensitivity. For some reason, at this point, I was still relatively calm, choosing to believe that whatever it was, UCLA could fix it, and I would be able to deal with it. It was the first time I was challenged to internalize the same positivity and guidance I had provided to many others for decades, to "walk the talk" and "wait to worry."

I don't remember much after arriving at UCLA early that Monday morning. I could not drive, so I spent the entire trip shielding my eyes from the sun and keeping them closed because I was now literally seeing two of everything. Janel had to physically and vocally guide me into the check-in and the waiting room. Janel was running point with the surgeon and the team of doctors, making all the decisions and keeping me calm. As I was being wheeled into pre-surgery prep, the last thing I remember was saying, "Honey, I love you." Janel will later confirm that I did say that, but I was also quite jovial and entertaining to the medical team. I remember waking up and seeing Janel at the side of my bed, surrounded by curtains and garbled voices. I felt like I was in a *Twilight Zone* episode. I could tell from her expression that everything had gone well, and I breathed a sigh of relief. I spent a week and a half at UCLA Medical Center post-surgery then was released to go home and wait for the biopsy results.

The craniotomy was performed on the right side of my skull just above my ear. The surgeon removed a portion of my skull about the size of a quarter. The goal was twofold, first to relieve the pressure on my brain and, indirectly, on my optical nerves. Something was causing inflammation of my meninges, specifically on my dura mater, one of the three layers of membranes that protect the brain and spinal cord. The second and more daunting purpose was to extract samples of the yellowish fluid to determine what it was and how best to treat it.

I took an extended leave of absence and remained at home, except for the occasional 45-minute trips to UCLA for post-surgery check-ins and updates on the biopsy status. Over the next three months, the dura mesh acted as a release valve. The inter-cranial swelling caused a Frankenstein-like bulge to occur on the side of my head. I remember venturing out to the grocery store and seeing the looks on people's faces, especially children, as I wobbled up and down the aisles. I was a shell of a man, but happy to be alive. Janel kept me from reeling into depression and wouldn't allow me to have a pity party, at least not for long. She took control, and I depended on her for everything. She checked the box on her portion of our "in sickness and in health" marriage vows.

It took three months for the UCLA Rheumatologist to determine the exact cause finally. During this period, my energy steadily decreased; I traded my regular glasses for my sunglasses even while sitting in the house. My appetite vanished, and my weight dropped from 205 to 178 pounds. It seemed my body was consuming itself. While I remained reasonably upbeat and positive, I have to admit the unknown was frightening at times. This was, after all, uncharted territory, but I was determined to wait to worry. We did not tell anyone in my family back in Texas for two weeks, because there was nothing to disclose. We didn't know what we were dealing with and wanted to wait until we did. We were us.

After a month after we decided it was time to bring everyone into the loop because the discovery process took longer than anticipated. My mom flew out to California to help take care of me for a couple of weeks while we anxiously waited for the biopsy results. She was instrumental in my recovery spiritually, emotionally, and by just being a mom. There are few things as special as the love between a mother and son. He loves his wife the best and his mother the longest. A blessed win-win situation.

Strategic Blessings

The chapter **My Journey** is devoted to the medical challenges that are the genesis for *59 Prime*. But this prelude bridges the role these exceptional individuals played at Dell and later at Amgen. I have been blessed professionally with amazing, strategically-placed mentors who have watched over me during my career. Here are three that mean the world to my family and me.

I joined Dell Technologies in the mid-1990s as a Financial Manager. I became friends with one of the P&L managers, David Johnston. After working together for a couple of years, David introduced me to his wife, Lori, who also worked there in Human Resources. The purpose was two-fold; he wanted us to meet because of our friendship, and because Lori wanted to create a new Metrics, Reporting, and Analysis position with the HR function. So we met, and I accepted the challenge, which was the beginning of an incredible personal and professional journey.

We have supported and comforted each other during the loss of siblings and have been a dynamic duo in executive settings. I am humbled to pick up the phone, send a text or email, and reach out to her whenever needed. I am one of many privileged to know Lori and am the beneficiary of her kindness and wisdom.

During my 2021 medical challenges, I used recovery downtime to reorganize and upgrade my work from home office space. As I shifted through some of the boxes of files I had kept as we moved from Austin to Simi Valley, California, and then back to Austin, I came across a clear folder. In it were pages of handwritten letters, neatly written using different colors to divide sections. I pulled one out dated April 26, 1998. It was from Lori, providing constructive feedback, words of encouragement, support, and development. I paused and read a few more. Even after 23 years, her words were motivating, challenging, and spot-on. In some ways, her demeanor and appearance were a professional version of my mom. Both are short in stature, but big in presence and impact.

At Dell, Lori introduced me to her boss, our HR SVP, Brian McNamee. Within minutes of the introduction, I knew my life and career would be forever changed. Brian was another senior HR leader who viewed the HR function and purpose from a business strategy and operations perspective. Both Lori and Brian would challenge and support me as I began to flex and infuse my Finance and business acumen into the traditional HR world. I became the Finance nerd within HR. I gained credibility within both functions by speaking both languages, building relationships, aligning their efforts, and acting as a strategic liaison.

In 2001, Brian left to pursue a new opportunity as the HR head of Amgen in California. He reached back and pulled a few of us along—specifically, Lori, Ted Bagley, and myself. At Dell, Ted led HR at our Nashville, Tennessee manufacturing facility. We became close friends and strategic partners because one of my direct reports was based in Nashville. Little did I know, that was just the beginning of another special bond.

I left Dell HR in 2002 and accepted a role as the Corporate Controller of Amgen. Brian, Lori, and Ted discussed a two-year career development plan for me, one that would allow me to build some credibility with the executive leadership and lead the Corporate Finance Planning and Analysis team. The goal would be to transition back into a strategic HR role ultimately.

Two years later, the plan was executed, and I assumed a role reporting to Ted as his Chief of Staff and HR Lead for Supply Chain, Engineering, and Process Development. Ted, too, took an active part in my career. He was coaching me through the challenges of being an African-American executive. He also reinforced my belief to see people first for who they are, not their race, gender, color, etc. Ted would also be the first person I reached out to when I had a seizure at work and couldn't remember Janel's number. During my recovery, I lost my appetite and was losing weight and mobility. Homebound, waiting for the biopsy results from UCLA, I spent most of my time on the couch wearing shades due to light sensitivity. Three weeks in, the doorbell rang. I slowly got up to answer it. I opened the door, and a gentleman stood there in a black suit. He said, "Michael Francis?" I said, "Yes sir." "I have a special delivery for you." I looked over his shoulder, and I saw a limo in the driveway. He handed me a big bag that said *Roscoe's Chicken and Waffles*. Brian and Ted knew I love Roscoe's and had this specially delivered from Gower Street in Los Angeles, some 45 miles away!

Amgen not only changed the trajectory of my life, it saved it. After being hospitalized four times in my life—two with potentially life-threatening consequences— and while waiting days for the final lab results and diagnosis, I had time, lots of it. Here's what I did then, and you can do now. Even today, I prioritize my life around my personal North Stars. There is no value in not sharing valuable life lessons. I wish I had done this sooner, and encourage you to do so now.

Then it happened, almost ninety days after the craniotomy. After ruling out cancer, tumors, Wagner's syndrome, Sarcoidosis, blood diseases, etc., my diagnosis had been narrowed down to a rare autoimmune disorder called Idiopathic Hypertrophic Cranial Pachymeningitis (IHCP). IHCP occurs when the dura mater becomes inflamed. IHCP onset results in chronic pressure being placed on the brain or spinal cord. When told about my rare diagnosis, I jokingly said to the Chief Neurosurgeon. "You know, my mom told me I was special. But I didn't want to be this special."

Going back to my statement earlier about the unknown benefit of our move to California and employment at Amgen: it was not until after the diagnosis, and further confirmed some six years later when we decided to return to Texas, that we would realize just how unique IHCP was and how fortunate it was for this diagnosis and treatment to happen near a facility such as UCLA. I engaged the UCLA team to identify an Austin health care facility with doctors familiar with treating IHCP. It took twenty-three attempts before we found one that had heard of, much less treated my condition. Our move to California, and the blessing of working for a fantastic company such as Amgen, had probably saved my life. To this day, I remain eternally grateful and have dozens of lifelong friends in Thousand Oaks, California

There is no cure for IHCP, so the next challenge would be for the UCLA team to identify an ongoing treatment regime that would effectively place this disorder into remission for the rest of my life. But first, an aggressive approach had to be taken to stop it dead in its tracks. This required the use of a high-dose steroid treatment regime.

Our bodies naturally create about five mg of Prednisone daily to help water absorption and control sodium levels. By contrast, my initial IHCP treatment regime consisted of 3,000 mg of Prednisone slowly infused over three days. The potential side effects from the extreme dosage were many, ranging from excessive swelling, disorientation, bone deterioration, aggressive behavior, and temporary loss of mobility. Going through this treatment was, figuratively, a journey in and of itself. Before beginning treatment, the Rheumatologist explained the pros, cons, and side effects. Steroids, especially in dosages at this level, can amplify a person's personality. If you are aggressive by nature, you will become more aggressive and might require leg and hand restraints to protect the patient and those attending to them. Then he asked Janel, "Does Michael exhibit any aggressive or other types of behavior?" She quickly responded, "No, he's a big teddy bear unless poked. The biggest problem you're problem going to have is keeping him quiet. He'll be polite and entertaining. "

After completing the steroid treatment, I quickly transitioned to chemotherapy and immunosuppressive therapies, receiving Cytoxan intravenously every three weeks for six months. Ultimately, it was determined that the best IHCP treatment for me would consist of a seven hundred milligram Remicade infusion every six weeks for the rest of my life. More than ten years later, I would come to understand the dire implications of deviating from that prescribed treatment regime

Since 2009, I've received my Remicade treatments, which I now refer to as my "Juicy Juice," regularly and with no subsequent IHCP flair-ups. Instead, my life, health, and outlook returned to normal to the point where I often forgot about the treatments or the illness until receiving an appointment reminder. Even today, getting those Remicade infusions is a helpful reminder of how far I've come, how precious life is, how things like this can happen to anyone at any time, and how blessed I am to be alive.

I purposely try to sit next to different individuals during my infusion sessions, striking up casual conversations, sharing a bit of myself in the hopes of making someone smile, laugh or provide a positive perspective or word. My success rate is pretty high, and I wind up internalizing some of the positivity that I was trying to give. It's a win-win situation! This rare autoimmune disorder might be one of the best gifts I have received thus far in my life. Humble pie won't let you get too full of yourself.

Hospitalization: Round Two

Soon after moving back to Texas in 2014, I developed a high sensitivity to allergies, often resulting in medically prescribed interventions. Something is always blowing around in the air: cedar, pollen, grass, ragweed, you name it, it thrives here. The main reason is due to the temperate climate. Plants in Texas only endure occasional periods of freezing temperatures, if any. This allows them to pollinate pretty much year-round, even in winter. So I, like many other Texans, are in a constant state of sniffling, coughing, and sneezing, and occasionally things escalate. More often than not, my seasonal allergies (winter and spring) can be quickly cured with a Z-pack and some mandatory rest and indoor restrictions.

The exception would be one time in January of 2019. I brought in the New Year a little more subdued than usual because my energy level was low. I continued to work from home but noticed that I was having trouble focusing and alternated between being slightly cold and excessively hot, and sweating profusely, often waking up in a pool of water. I started checking my temperature and noticed it would spike to 100 degrees plus, then quickly come down to normal. I did not want to take any chances, so I set up an appointment with my primary care physician, thinking it was time for another Z-Pack and rest. I got both, but things got worse. After a weekend trip to the emergency room, I was directed to return to my primary care physician immediately on Monday. I was, by my standards, noticeably weaker and thinner.

As I waited in the doctor's office lobby on Monday, I remember telling Janel, "I'm burning up and having difficulty breathing. I know my temperature is at least 102 degrees!" So I went back and did the regular check-in routine, stood on the scale, and was shocked. I had lost twenty-one pounds in twenty-six days, and I was wrong about my temperature. It was actually 104 degrees, at which point the nurse said, "We are checking you into the hospital immediately." A wheelchair appeared, and I was whisked to the emergency room.

I would spend the next week hospitalized and receiving treatment for pneumonia with a touch of bronchitis. Fluids, antibiotics, and rest were the prescribed treatment. So here I was after eleven years, back again in a hospital gown and hooked up to an IV drip. I had nothing but time—and lots of it—to think about my life, blessings, and what was important to me. I worked on a presentation that morning to make sure I followed through on my deliverables and commitments. I remember laying in the bed and thinking, "What the heck am I doing to myself?" Here I am practically working myself to death, some self-induced, and some part of the corporate mentality. I realized at that moment how quickly and easily we can all be replaced professionally, but not personally. An even deeper thought occurred to me: how many headstones listed a person's profession? I couldn't think of many. I had inadvertently put my work ahead of my life. It was time for a change. I needed to reshuffle the deck in my favor, and play on my terms and with my priorities.

During my weeklong stay, Janel again took the reins making the decisions and daily treks from our house to the hospital to spend time and sleep in the chair next to me. There are no words to express how I feel, but I call her "Angel" for multiple reasons. I was released from the hospital after a week, but was then required to go on short-term disability for at least two months to regain my strength and fully heal. Then I returned to work, and within two months, I left corporate America from a full-time employee standpoint and began pursuing it from a management advisory frame of mind. More to come later about my transition plan and new career.

Hospitalization: Round Three

Fast forward two years later to January 2021. My New Year's resolution for 2021 was to begin getting myself fit for the big 60. I went all-in on improving my mental health and wellness. I completed a 21-day internal cleanse, increased my distance from 2.1 to 3.2 miles a day, and cut out alcohol, sugar, bread, and soda. The results were impressive! I lost 14 pounds in less than a month. However, I didn't realize that God was giving me the time to prepare physically, spiritually, and emotionally and allowing me to prepare for some serious hand-to-hand combat right around the corner that I could not foresee coming.

I officially launched my own business, BEAM, in September of 2020. In January, my insurance coverage transitioned to a new provider. Because my diagnosis is considered a rare disorder, the new provider had not heard of it and was hesitant to approve the Remicade treatment and the associated costs ($9,000 per session). The delays continued as my Rheumatologist office and the insurance company exchanged questions, information, and emails. There was lots of back and forth. Each week I'd check on the status as I was beginning to experience some tingling and blurriness in my left eye. I knew that was where the initial IHCP symptoms manifested itself thirteen years ago. One week turned into two, two into three, and three into four.

I continued my regular routine, working, researching, meeting with clients, preparing presentations, participating in Zoom meetings, driving to appointments, running errands, etc. Sound familiar? Old habits are hard to break. However, I couldn't help but notice that the vision in my left eye was starting to deteriorate to the point it was beginning to impact my job performance. My body was beginning to go through withdrawals from not receiving the Remicade every six weeks as prescribed. This delay was fast approaching the time when I would be preparing for my subsequent treatment. This was uncharted territory.

By February, looking through my left eye, I could no longer clearly focus on objects. Instead, only fluid shapes in a kaleidoscope of colors, moving back and forth like waves. My peripheral vision had become blurred, and like a curtain, it descended from the top of my eye gradually downward. Over these four weeks, the curtain slowly dropped from 25% to 50% and eventually 75% visual impairment. Meanwhile, my right eye was operating overtime as I tried my best to make the most of the situation. I did not share what was happening broadly or proactively with anyone. But I knew a medical intervention would be required because this situation was not going to self-correct.

After a four-week delay, my Remicade treatment had finally been scheduled for Friday, February 12th. Unfortunately, the morning of the 12th, I received an email informing me that all non-essential medical treatments had been canceled. All non-life-threatening procedures and business operations were shutting down due to the arrival of a historic Texas ice storm, which was later referred to as SNOVID-21. I informed my Rheumatologist of the cancellation and the drastic changes in my vision. He immediately put me on a 60mg daily dose of Prednisone and would reassess things on Monday to determine the next steps.

I spent Saturday through Monday night at home without power, with temperatures dipping below 40 degrees inside, and below zero outside. I remained active and pretty positive on social media. It was my only form of external communication, and although it was becoming difficult to focus or read, it took my mind off of what was happening. No one knew but Janel, who was out of town taking care of her parents, and my brother Brian. At this point, there was nothing to tell and nothing anyone could do but worry. That's something I did not want to happen.

Time alone with your thoughts can be a good thing. For some reason, even in the cold, I knew things would be okay. I doubled down on my prayers, not necessarily for resolution, but for the blessings I had received during the past 59 years: loving and amazing parents, a strong sibling bond, 35 years of being married to an incredible woman, friends on every continent except Antarctica, a successful career, and more importantly, an eternally optimistic approach to life and friendships.

I could handle the cold, but I knew that not having full vision under these conditions was not an ideal situation. On Monday, I texted my doctor and informed him things were getting progressively worse. On Tuesday, a decision was made to go to the emergency room and check into the hospital for treatment. He prescribed the same treatment I received thirteen years ago at UCLA: 3,000 mgs of Prednisone infused over three days.

Early Tuesday morning, a neighbor with a four-wheel drive Jeep drove me through the two-foot-high snowdrifts to the emergency room. The first day, I spent ten hours in the waiting room, as this snowstorm was wreaking havoc on Texas. People with broken bones, sprains, and collision-related incidents were ahead of and all around me. While waiting in the lobby for my name to be called, I dialed into a weekly team meeting, engaging quietly and sporadically. No one on the call was aware that I was participating from the emergency room lobby. I remained positive on social media, and honestly, I'm not sure if my responses and posts were meant for someone else or intended for me. The reality of what was and what was about to happen was finally beginning to sink in.

I spent the first night sleeping on a gurney in the hall because there were no regular rooms available. The nurse told me that my brain MRI had was scheduled for 9:00 pm. An attendant would be coming to take me to the MRI area via wheelchair. Later, as I watched the technician prepare and discuss the process, one I had undergone more than three dozen times before, I struck up a conversation with him. First medically, "Is this going to be with or without contrast?" Then the conversation migrated to more personal topics, "How long have you been doing this?" Next, "Are you from Austin?" Eventually, the conversation made its way around to food!

In the spring of 2020, I started a Facebook food page called *EpicuriousThe1*. I've shared my recipes, over 500 pictures, cooking techniques, Live videos of me grilling, and my favorite places to dine. At this writing, I have over 300 followers, some located in Canada, Asia, South America, and Europe. By the time I was getting strapped in for the MRI, and he had inserted the IV, we had become pretty good friends, and he was also pretty hungry from looking at pictures of my cooking prowess. It was an impactful but straightforward conversation initiated by my love of all things food. When the procedure concluded, I thanked him for being attentive and for the great conversation. Before falling asleep in the hallway, I glanced at my phone to check messages, LinkedIn, and social media. He too was now a follower of *EpicuriousThe1*. I smiled, then drifted off to sleep.

On the second day, upon arriving at my room, I was informed that the septic system had frozen and toilets were no longer operating. As a result, all patients have been asked to utilize wastebaskets. I responded, "Ok, cool, what else you got?" I had trained for this on Kilimanjaro, the Himalayas, and on the Inca Trail. The nurse smiled and said, "They said it probably wouldn't phase you!"

The days leading up to and then being in the hospital were blessings in disguise. Lots of quality time to think and reflect on my life and what impact I had or could have on the lives of others. This was now my second time receiving this type of treatment, but what about those who needed it and would never get a chance to receive it due to financial or economic circumstances, or just being born in a different place or continent? I realized how blessed I was and was determined to share and hopefully inspire others going into or coming out of a personal storm.

I completed the Prednisone treatment and was released from the hospital on Thursday evening. Power had been restored, so I was excited to be going home. Janel returned home, and I received some good news the next day (Friday). My Remicade treatment had been rescheduled for Monday, some five weeks later than prescribed. After receiving the treatment, I realized that my vision was not improving. Again, I contacted my Rheumatologist, who then quickly recommended I contact my Ophthalmologist.

On Tuesday morning, I met with my Ophthalmologist. He performed a series of visual scans and tests and then paused. I had seen that pause before. He asked, "How long have you been operating with this impaired vision in your left eye?"

I responded, "Since the beginning of the year, so about 5-weeks." He said, "Michael, you have a detached retina in your left eye and need emergency surgery." I said, "Ok, let's do it." It seemed pretty logical to me. If something is broken and is capable of being fixed, get it fixed. I was blessed to have insurance to cover the procedure, so why postpone, complain or debate? There are lots of people who would love to be in my position.

I met with the optical surgeon on Wednesday morning. He showed me images of the three retinal tears, talked about the procedure and pre-and post-surgery actions. The detachment most likely occurred due to time and opportunity--time being my age, and opportunity being the delayed Remicade treatment. This was probably going to happen sometime in the future; it just happened a little sooner. I had two partial and one major retinal detachment.

The major tear was the primary area of concern because it was located on the bottom of my retina. Its primary function is to act as a stabilizer for my eyeball, keeping my eye from moving around uncontrollably. The procedure required inserting a scleral buckle to support my retina, giving the tears time to heal and hopefully supporting my eye in the usual way as before. The surgery was scheduled and completed the next day, Thursday evening. Things were happening quickly! Per our standard operating protocol, I deferred everything to Janel, and I don't remember much. While being prepped for surgery, I told her, "Honey, so they'll be putting in a squirrel buckle or something like that in my eye. So I'll be like the Bionic Man when I come out of surgery." What I do remember is all of the extra COVID-19 precautions that were in place at the hospital. I had to get a COVID-19 test that morning, and there were safety protocols and checkpoints right up until I was being wheeled in for surgery. Talk about being in a sterile environment.

The following week, I had my second follow-up appointment with the surgeon. I arrived early, had my temperature checked at the desk, and found a seat in the lobby. I began talking to a lady sitting on my right about "Snovid." The guy behind us chimed in. The conversation was a combination of frustration and survival stories. After a few minutes, an elderly lady on my left joined in as well. The tone had changed from sadness and finger-pointing to optimism and camaraderie. Finally, my name was called, and as I headed back to see the doctor, the attendant said, "Wow! Look at that! Your empty chair is in the middle, and four people sitting around it, who don't know each other, are talking like they've known each other. Strangers don't usually do that." I looked over, then smiled warmly, and responded to her, "Strangers are only people who haven't met. It's a small world if you take the time to talk to people."

Two weeks after retinal surgery, I was able to remove the patch. My vision was still blurry, but my right eye allowed me to function reasonably well. I finally had the opportunity to watch *The Book of Eli* with Janel for the first time start to finish. It was moving, inspiring, spiritual and humbling. Lying in bed, watching the movie credits run, I gazed out the window. Suddenly, tears began to stream down my face, and I started sobbing. I told Janel, "Honey, I can see trees. I can see the trees and the limbs." Up until then, all I could see were colors and patterns.

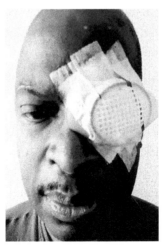

By mid-March, the vision in my left eye had improved from legally blind to 80/20. Simultaneously, I began the long process of slowly being weaned off the high Prednisone dosage. I had been able to function amazingly well while averaging around 40mg daily. But when it drops below 20mg, I was warned that because of how much steroids my body had absorbed during this treatment, I would probably experience some withdrawal symptoms. As a result, it would take another 3-4 months before I was ultimately off of steroids. By this point, I had received more than 5,000 mg of Prednisone, or an average of 80mgs, per day.

A month after my initial hospital stay, I knew it was time to bring my immediate family into the loop about what had transpired. Due to COVID-19, this was the first time my family was able to be together under that same roof in five months. It was an emotional and sobering gathering. We knew other families would never reunite or would do so with empty chairs around their table.

I asked everyone to have a seat. First, I thanked my parents for instilling so much faith, hope, and resiliency in me. Then I shared everything that had transpired during the past month. There were tears, bowed heads, solemn gestures, silent and vocal prayers. My brother Tony was a little angry with me for not telling them sooner. I responded, "I'm not going to apologize for not allowing you to cry and worry unnecessarily for 28 days. I love you all too much to do that." There was just no compelling reason to share this sooner, and I believed that doing it in person was the right approach. My logic was:

1. The cause was known and had happened before.
2. I knew the prognosis and treatment.

3. Others in my family we're dealing with much worse.
4. It occurred during the snowstorm.
5. There was absolutely nothing anyone could do when it was happening other than worry.

Being hospitalized twice within six days gives you a new perspective on this thing called life. My mental, professional, emotional, physical, and spiritual outlook changed for the better, and all to share what I had experienced, internally and externally. I was starting to get excited by what I had learned and my hopes for writing *59 Prime*. Up until now, I had only shared bits and pieces of the journey and, even then, the G-rated version. I've never been one to complain, which is good and bad. Not doing so can result in people minimizing or normalizing what you are going through. There were times when I felt that way.

Occasionally, when asked to do things beyond my current physical capability due to my post-op medical treatments, I had to remind people, "You do realize that I only have partial vision in one eye," or "Yep, I have put on a few pounds because I've been on an extremely high dose of steroids for four months." That's the downside of carrying your burden well. Yet still, I unequivocally remain committed to walking the talk, saying less, doing more, forgiving more, inspiring more, and sharing my story. I've seen the amazing fruit that hope, optimism, perseverance, positivity, and faith can bear.

As part of my post-op recovery, I decided to unplug from social media until further along in this journey. For me, one of the downsides of being on Prednisone was my inability to stop myself from responding to stimuli. I didn't want to exert or devote any energy to the divisive political climate,

COVID-19, racial turmoil, and the perpetual dark clouds. Less is better. Besides, there was nothing new in world news; the central themes and issues have never changed. Even today, I no longer watch the news or any other non-value add media—one of the best habits I have adopted since turning 59.

I halted all professional obligations and began to focus on getting better holistically. I decided to set up a home office at my parents' house, not just for an additional workspace but also for a comfortable place to escape from the urban stresses and enjoy the country views. But more importantly, I wanted to spend more time with, and help take care of my parents. Time was moving on, and neither my parents nor myself are getting younger. Initially, I spent a week and a half there, providing more clarity and life reflections. The breadth and depth of my writing increased exponentially. I went from scribbling thoughts on 2"x2" to 4"x6" to eventually 6"x 8" size Post-It notes, fast and furious at times. I didn't spend much time editing, just capturing thoughts and words, as I knew I wouldn't remember most of them the next day or week.

Food seemed to be a catalyst for my creativity. Something as simple as making a peanut butter sandwich could take 40 minutes. Something extraordinary was happening. I knew it was not of my own doing, as I was not capable of this type of rapid creativity and expression. But fortunately, for once, I was smart enough not to question it and just let it flow. After sharing bits and pieces of my journey and what I had captured with others, I felt it might be inspiring or helpful to others.

Even today, my Rheumatologist and Optical surgeon don't fully understand how I continued to function normally during those five months on such a high level of steroids and a detached retina—all while maintaining such a positive outlook and being more concerned about enlightening and uplifting others. To this day, I believe that no matter how bad things are, there's always someone who is going through much worse, and given the chance, they would gladly exchange places with you. By weathering these storms, I believe I am a living example of what faith can do. I know I have been blessed and believe I have an obligation to share my story with others.

I am stronger and more humble, reflective, optimistic, peaceful, and grateful because of what I went through in 2008, 2019, and 2021. I hope that sharing my story will help support others currently at a peak or in the valley of their personal journey. You don't need to understand everything that happens in life. Sometimes, you have to trust what you see, feel, and believe in your core.

Throughout this recent experience, it was as if I was cloaked in a calm sense of spiritual comfort and confidence. Now, my thoughts and mind are more at ease, more transparent and genuine when I'm at my parent's house, and even more so in the room where my brother Tweety transitioned. I guess there's some truth to the phrase "There's no place like home." When I am there, not a day goes by without a new, humbling revelation or blessing.

When you are late in the third quarter of life, your thoughts and words become more reflective and your actions more intentional. You quickly filter out the noise in the world and instinctively focus on what you can control and the items in your top five. Because at this point in the game of life, every shot counts.

In March through April 2021, my vision improved from being legally blind to 20/60. However, in the next three months, the scar tissue gradually began to obstruct more and more of my vision. I knew there would be at least one more surgery to fully restore my vision. By the end of July, it had deteriorated to 20/200. To be clear, coming out of the initial dark clouds in 2021 was not easy. In July, while in the final stages of recovery, I was diagnosed with mild depression. The combination of a year and a half of Covid-19 self-imposed social distancing due to my compromised immune system, being hospitalized twice within six days, the residual effects of a six-month high dose steroid treatment and its subsequent withdrawal symptoms, and trying to return to some sense of normalcy had taken a toll. These were more reasons to seek inner peace and narrow my focus.

By August, my daily Prednisone dosage had decreased from a peak of 60 mg to 4 mg, and I was starting to feel like my old self, only 30 pounds heavier. My appetite and eating habits returned to normal. I knew things were starting to look up when I felt that old familiar urge to put some meat on the pits! I hadn't done that since the week before the snowstorm in February. There is no better way to get yourself out of a funk than doing things that you enjoy. So I brined three racks of beef ribs, some carnitas (pork shoulder), two turkey breasts, and a whole chicken. Believe it or not, that's not a big cookout by my standards, but it was a start. Talk about being therapeutic!

Step two was to resume exercising. I slowly started working out again, first with light weights and by taking short walks. Muscle memory is a good thing, and there's nothing like working up an honest sweat, some soreness, and a few body aches.

I scheduled my final eye surgery for Monday, August 16th. I approached it the same way as the first. Outside of Janel, I was engaging initially only with my brother Brian. If it ain't broke, don't fix it—no need to unnecessarily worry my parents or other family members.

The 45-minute optical surgery was considered non-life-threatening. I was excited about the prospect of regaining clarity in my left eye. In some respects, the surgery was successful, but it also created and accelerated a few new challenges. The multiple surgeries had taken a toll on my eyes, and I would need cataract surgery in a couple of months to reap the full benefits.

As I finish compiling the final chapters of this book, it is now the end of September. I learned that my doctor did a little more than scar tissue removal at my post-op appointment. My cornea and sclera had been cleaned, and some other potential stressors had been eliminated. As the attendant removed the bandages from my eye, I could feel and see the difference relative to the first surgery. It healed much quicker compared to the previous two surgeries.

I completed my transition off the high-dose steroid treatment the last week of August and felt my body returning to its regular cadence. My energy, motivation, and enthusiasm for life and people returned. My conviction and commitment to give and be more, dare I say, are "on steroids." Time is of the essence, and I am optimistic about what I can be at 60 and beyond. When things change, they change. So I'm moving with a purpose, trying to approach each day with the intent to touch someone positively.

You don't go through these life events without some growth, humility, and reflection. They remain aspirational guideposts.

I know I've got some work to do. Though the dark clouds no longer hover above, they are just around the corner. I've got to up my game, focus less on material things, listen less to my internal demons, say less, listen more, try to give more, uplift more, invest in others more, and make more time for those who have played a significant role in my life. I plan to expand my current core network just a bit more. I have received many incredible gifts in the past 59 years. Hopefully, by continuing to share mine, they will plant seeds of hope and inspiration that multiply and bear fruit.

This truly has been a journey for me, but I am also aware of others who have endured much more and would love to be in my shoes. Life happens; no one is immune. It's ok to feel broken, but it's not ok to stay broken. Seek help. I did, and you can too, so please do. It is not a sign of weakness, it's an act of redemption for life's warriors. Our wounds can and do heal, and we can share lessons learned and words of encouragement with others, which I am doing with *59 Prime*.

I have been asked: "So, what happened to you? I mean, you were always pretty positive, but now it feels, looks, and sounds a little different!" Well, honestly, life happened to me. I no longer seek to understand or analyze it. Now, I am fully committed to embracing it, and more importantly, paying it forward. There is no value if these life blessings and gifts leave this earth with me. If only one of them resonates with someone, meets and helps them in their time of need, or inspires someone else to share more about their journey, I will be grateful to have played a small role in facilitating someone's enlightenment, triumph, or happiness.

Occasionally we have to be reminded that we are not always in control of every aspect of our life. After my third eye surgery, my surgeon cleared me to return to the original Ophthalmologist, who identified the initial retinal detachment back in February. My vision and recovery were at a point where it was time to assess my new glasses prescription. I was looking forward to seeing him, thanking him, and letting him know that I was on the other side of that storm. On October 1st, I arrived at the appointment cautiously optimistic, understanding that the vision in my left eye had been compromised, and a more intense prescription would probably be required. I felt I probably would test between 20/60 or 20/80. After bouncing back from being "legally blind," I'd be happy with whatever life dictated. Besides, that's what glasses are for, to correct impaired vision.

Well, I was pretty spot on with the diagnosis. But what I wasn't anticipating was the new retinal tear that had developed, this time in my right eye. This time, it was not as severe as my first tear, but it, too, required immediate attention. I paused after taking in this new information. I took a deep breath and gave the thumbs up. Thirty minutes later, I was prepped and sitting in the chair waiting for laser surgery. After the 2nd dilation, it was showtime. One hundred and ninety-seven laser blasts later, it was done. So much for me thinking that this part of **My Journey** was winding down. I now fully realized that I'd be coming back periodically to deal with the side effects of the intense surgeries, and in time, cataracts.

As I sat in the lobby afterwards, letting my eyes re-adjust to the light. I remember thinking, *Boy, how quickly things can change*. I walked in here for a new prescription, and an hour later, I'm recovering from a laser treatment on my so-called "good eye." Wow! Just because you feel you're done with parts of your life doesn't mean that life is done with you. Maybe this was just another reminder and test to see if I believed in the advice, optimism, and faith that I had poured into *59 Prime*. I absolutely do.

During the entire ordeal, I didn't bat an eye (no pun intended). When my Optometrist said it required surgery, I said, "Well, let's do it." When he said, "I'm almost done," I said, "Take your time, make sure you get it all." Afterward, he said, "I wish all my patients were as resilient, optimistic, and easy-going as you." I just smiled and thought things happen for a reason, more *59 Prime* challenges and triumphs. For me, the contents of this book were already serving a purpose. Without realizing it, I was already leaning on it.

These are just a few life moments that made 2021 a reflective, humbling, and inspiring year, providing more proof that life is ever-evolving with many twists and turns and waits for no one. Each of us gets to choose: remain stagnant, or evolve based on our life experiences. For me, I will now focus my energy on those things that I believe I will miss the most during my last days on earth.

In the following two chapters, you'll find 59 hope and inspirational reflections and 59 career and life lessons. These are not musings that I have by no means mastered, but they serve as inspirational reminders. So make a note of those that resonate with you for future reference.

CHAPTER 6

HOPE & INSPIRATION

"There are two ways of spreading light: to be the candle or the mirror that reflects it."—Edith Wharton

Hope and inspiration can give us the confidence to face life's most painful moments and not only survive but thrive. Here are 59 realizations and reflections I wanted to share with you.

1. The gift of a smile, hug, word of encouragement, or act of kindness has NO expiration date. Our treasure boxes are filled with an unlimited amount of these precious gems to distribute.

2. Recognize and acknowledge your gifts and blessings. They are NOT promised, should NOT be expected, and are NOT permanent.

3. There's no better moment to speak about faith than when you are in the midst of the squall. Those torrential

thunderstorms become less ominous with time and distance. They quickly fade from sight and mind.

4. Our responses and actions during times of tragedy, death, or dire circumstances reveal our true core. They shine a bright light on what is "real" and what is "aspirational."

5. In addition to time, our existence also dissipates "in the twinkling of an eye."

6. Not all friends need or should be considered close friends. Develop barriers of entry. Preserve, protect and manage your core confidants. The ones who are with you, always.

7. Each day that we rise, we are writing history. May your penmanship be good and your words true.

8. Always be you. Be you always; I recommend doing both, ALWAYS.

9. It might be possible to have a surplus of blessings, faith, and optimism. If you find yourself in this enviable position, please consider an aggressive inventory reduction strategy. There's ALWAYS someone in desperate need of your excess capacity.

10. Activate this inspirational state of mind and archive it with your other natural impulses: Always aspire to leave people in a better place than where you found them.

11. Start living, not talking about, the life you want people to associate you with when you are gone.

12. During challenging times, visualize how you want to feel and be seen when you come out on the other side. Because 99.99% of the time, you will survive.

13. Focus on what you CAN control, your:
    *   Time

- Health and wellness
- Words
- Actions
- Outlook

14. Always take pride in your work. Always go above and beyond. Always treat everyone with respect.

15. About negativity: DON'T allow yourself to absorb it. Instead, take frequent mental breaks from non-valuable noise. Be reflective, spend more quality time with your loved ones, and reclaim your zen.

16. Hate is a contagious, opportunistic, and stealthy virus. Avoid it at ALL costs. Be careful not to become what you INGEST. Love is ALWAYS a better option.

17. It's difficult to be genuinely happy for others if you are NOT genuinely happy with yourself first.

18. DO NOT let life zoom by because you spent too much time trying to dissect and analyze it.

19. Change, for some, oscillates somewhere between improbable and impossible. Personal growth requires self-awareness.

20. Time management is the one common but unique superpower that we all possess. Allocate it wisely.

21. Things change! If you have drawn some lines in the sand years or decades ago that still exist today, I strongly encourage you to revisit each one and contemplate if now is the time to wash a few of them away.

22. Life is precious and fleeting. My advice: don't procrastinate. You had better hurry!

23. Ground yourself in faith sooner rather than later. Dark clouds are a necessary and reoccurring part of life.

24. B.O.L.O. is a commonly used law enforcement term meaning "be on the lookout." I believe the acronym has a powerful motivational meaning as well: be open-hearted and live optimistically.

25. Nobody owns the rights to kindness, encouragement, inspiration, compassion, or trust. These are universally available for optimum utilization. They remain individual choices.

26. Often that which remains unspoken is more important than what has already been said.

27. DO NOT become so fixated and inflexible with time management that you forget to enjoy it, especially if the restrictions are self-imposed.

28. There's a natural order to acceptance. Unfortunately, it can be difficult for someone to believe what is being said if they cannot comprehend or empathize with the messenger's journey.

29. Be kind to all. Go above and beyond for those you care about. Be a life catalyst. Help set things in motion. It is not wasted energy. Remember, everything is circular.

30. When those dark clouds become visible on the horizon, please know that not all of them will reach your shore. Remember and practice these three simple but powerful words: wait to worry.

31. Please DO NOT question a blessing. Instead, always acknowledge and appreciate it for what it is—a gift.

32. DO NOT let others struggle through situations that you have survived. Instead, tap into your personal iCloud, download, share, and support them.

33. Each of us has a unique and personal story to tell and gifts to give.

34. In the short term, real help can unintentionally and temporarily hurt. So, ask for it from those you love, respect, and trust. Then, at least, you're assured it is being given from a place of genuine concern, care, and honesty.

35. Never be sorry for being you. Each of us is special, unique, and quirky by design.

36. In life, there will always be at least two lanes on which to travel, regardless of speed, direction, duration, or gradient. There is always a high and a low road from which we can choose.

37. Never dim your light because it's too bright for some. If they choose to remain in your life, then kindly recommend that they might need to wear sunglasses.

38. Aspire to change the world by just being you. Even if you fall short, you'll have left nothing on the playing field. I'm aware of someone who achieved worldwide eminence in approximately 33 short years.

39. Sleep is not a developmental opportunity for most. So live life now and to the fullest. Each of us will have the opportunity to sleep peacefully in eternity.

40. Learn to accept positive and negative outcomes gracefully. You will experience both; you will evolve and survive. Catalog your experiences under wisdom.

41. I've learned to value and actively seek opportunities to engage intimately with my faith and silence.

42. Sometimes walking the path of life can be difficult, lonely, and humbling, but it's another example of faith under construction.

43. We are all human. Don't be too quick to pass judgment, determining guilt or innocence. My mom will be quick to remind you, "Baby, that's somebody's child."

44. Learn to exercise patience. Watch the ebb and flow of things. Don't waste precious time and energy—only paddle when it makes sense.

45. Sometimes feedback and truth can be hard to digest. However, if the source is credible and the gift sincere, its long-term value is priceless.

46. Our outer shells will eventually deteriorate. However, it's our essence that has unlimited potential, beauty, and longevity.

47. Most of my friendships evolved from simple but genuine comments and gestures: "Hi, I'm Michael, how are you doing?" "Are you OK? Really nice to meet you!" or "Ooh, I've heard a lot of good things about you!" There are others, and all are free, simple, and time-tested.

48. The odds of success exponentially increase when we focus on those things strategically positioned within our strike zone. Understand your strengths, and leverage them accordingly.

49. Overcoming adversity builds muscle memory into life's portfolio. We acquire new tools, perspectives, and techniques for future reference and develop the confidence to continue moving forward.

50. Actions ALWAYS speak louder than words, especially in life, love, leadership, and legacy.

51. There is a stark difference between being a work in process and being aspirational. If you focus on the first one, the second will begin to shrink over time.

52. Hard work and wealth are often considered to be close relatives. Their kinship is inextricably woven together by perceived interdependence. But in terms of value or sequential lineage, always view wealth as hard work's third or fourth cousin.

53. Watch what people do versus what they say they'll do. In some cases, their actions confirm that their words were just aspirational proclamations.

54. Give little or no credence to those who are uncomfortable with your self-improvement efforts. There is a strong possibility that they might lack self-awareness.

55. We can change the world simply by striving to be the best possible version of ourselves.

56. Life happens without notice, explanation, or apology. No one is immune. When things change, then things change.

57. Inflexibility limits possibilities, potential, and personal growth.

58. There are unquantifiable benefits for constantly infusing increasing flexibility into your life, especially when managing health, wellness, time, and spirituality.

59. Optimize every second, minute, hour, and day of your existence. I don't think it is wise to procrastinate against an unknown stopwatch and undefeated foe. Time is an unrivaled and impartial opponent.

CHAPTER 7

CAREER & LIFE LESSONS

*"I've learned that making a 'living' is not
the same thing as making a 'life.'"—Maya Angelou*

I have also learned hundreds of poignant and invaluable lessons in the past 59 years. I believe I've learned something from everyone I've met along my journey. Some lessons were learned the hard way, some through observation, but most from adhering to a simple phrase known as The Golden Rule: *"Treat people like you would want to be treated."* Here are a few **Career and Life Lessons**. Most are interchangeable guideposts I strive to utilize in my personal and professional life.

1. DO NOT let anyone alter your story to make it easier to justify or digest.

2. Leadership 101: With authority comes great responsibility. Irrational or biased decision-making can have dire and unintended consequences for those under your charge.

3. You cannot outsource your legacy. So, get busy creating it.

4. Sometimes we have to fall off the train only to realize we have been traveling on the wrong set of tracks.

5. Stress and duress are rigorous and necessary leadership calibration tools.

6. You can keep yourself mentally fit, humble, and grounded by maintaining an adequate amount of distance between yourself and the spotlight.

7. One's value can be calibrated by what does or does not happen during their absence.

8. It is not your job to convince someone to change. Unfortunately, some are too deeply entrenched to embrace support. Respect their choice.

9. When you are wrong, own it and make it right.

10. WARNING: Hypocrisy thrives during times of controversy, chaos, and crisis.

11. Positivity is a powerful weapon—exercise caution on when, where, and how it is deployed. If not authentically communicated, it increases doubt and will deliver diminishing long-term returns.

12. DO NOT pursue things with artificially inflated, materialistic, or diminishing value, especially if that thing is money.

13. DO NOT alter your message or yourself when provided with a bigger platform. Even today, these old phrases ring

true: "Dance with the one who brought you," and "If it ain't broke, don't fix it."

14. DO NOT ridicule or judge someone capable of communicating in a different language. Speaking multiple dialects is a gift, not a curse.

15. Just because something has been recognized as a tradition does not necessarily make it appropriate in the present. Occasionally, it is a healthy endeavor to challenge the status quo. Doing so has been the foundation of evolution.

16. Be suspicious of those who vehemently condemn or reject the obvious or facts, but quickly reverse position based solely on the messenger. They are inconsistent individuals at best, and toxic cohorts at worst.

17. Normalization is often an impulsive or strategic self-defense mechanism. Instead, learn to accept facts, even if you struggle to wrap your head around them. By definition, truth is always fact-based.

18. Exercise caution around those who shy away from or question the duration or validity of positivity and sunshine, especially if they are most comfortable or at their best living under dark or cloudy skies.

19. In track and field, as well as life, DO NOT spend a disproportionate amount of time thinking about clearing hurdles #3, #4, or #5. It's good to be strategic, but it's critical to conquer the hurdle directly before you, lest the others will not exist.

20. Exercise caution before passing judgment. Always ask yourself: 1. Does this impact me? 2. Is it hurtful? 3. Is it necessary? 4. Who am I to judge?

21. Many times, we are our biggest roadblock.

22. When it comes to parental care or requests, I respond without hesitation, expectation, consternation, altercation, interrogation, or obligation. It should be an honor, not a burden or inconvenience.

23. It's in our darkest hours that the brightest of lights shine on our character.

24. I have learned to pause before speaking or taking action. Not everything is as it first appears to be.

25. Responsibility, ownership, and accountability are different but synonymous terms. If you acquire or accept one by default, you inherit them all.

26. Push back hard when someone attempts to hold you to a standard much higher than they are capable of meeting.

27. Often, when someone puts the shoe on the other foot, they finally realize it DOES NOT fit.

28. CAUTION: Choose wisely. If you overindulge in or regularly absorb something, you can become or emulate it.

29. "Some problems you have to have and some you don't." Wisdom by Marshall Francis

30. Periodically, we all need to upgrade our internal operating systems. Windows 97 will not run very efficiently, if at all, in today's ever-changing world.

31. Consider focusing on things you can control, things that make you happy, and the people you care about, because that is all that matters.

32. When you prioritize your words, you prioritize your actions. Instead of a work-life balance, we should strive for a life-work balance.

33. About preparing ourselves for death: we know not when it comes. My advice: Don't just get ready, stay ready.

34. If you think about it, how much daily or headline news is new? How much of it makes you upset or depressed? And how much of it can you change? Be judicious; your time here is unknown.

35. Time is non-refundable. Encourage people to sort out any questions they might have about your motives on their own time, not yours, and preferably by themselves. After all, that might be where their real struggle exists.

36. Invest heavily in people you love and care about. We rise by lifting others.

37. Start with the basics. Say "Hi," smile, be kind, or listen to someone. Doing so can forever change their life and your life.

38. Everything reveals itself at the proper time and place. The truth will eventually prevail.

39. While the what will always be relevant, the how is the more important lever. It's the directive and action that builds trust and loyalty and defines legacies.

40. Problems are a perpetual and integral part of life—no need to create one because one currently does not exist. There is always another one waiting impatiently right around the corner.

41. Determination, ambition, compassion, and integrity are not teachable character attributes. They do or do not exist.

42. It is not your job to convince all non-believers. Respect their position. It is a personal choice often referred to as disbelief.

43. In life, sometimes it is best to stay out of the kitchen and away from the dinner table, especially when the main course is being seasoned with putrid, bitter, and divisive spices.

44. Don't let people slow you down just because they can't keep up.

45. Remember, you can only control or participate on one side of a transaction or communication process. So pick a side, and regardless of the outcome, stay tethered to it.

46. Sometimes it is best to be quiet and keep your thoughts to yourself. Gather data, but stay above the fray. Remember, nonsense makes no sense.

47. Not everything in life arrives in completed form. Sometimes you have to look at things not as they are, but for what they could be. That goes for ourselves as well.

48. Each of us gets to decide how we spend our time. DO NOT waste a second of it responding to those who question what you choose to do with yours.

49. There is no substitute for taking action.

50. When accomplishments exceed expectations, the results are transparent, and usually speak for themselves. Never praise yourself too loudly, or let others downplay your achievements.

51. When "What's the rush?" becomes a legitimate question, then asking "What's the delay?" or "What are the barriers or roadblocks?" become valid inquiries or responses. The reverse is true as well.

52. Be leery of those who throw personal or professional darts, but protect or do not possess their own moral dartboard.

53. Unfortunately, even acts of kindness require courage and conviction. If a doubter asks, "Now, why did you do that?" look them straight in the eye and respond, "Well, why didn't you?" or "Because you wouldn't."

54. Pause. A reflective response is usually far superior to a knee-jerk reaction.

55. When NOT acknowledged, corrected, or atoned for, mistakes, history, and injustice are destined to be repeated.

56. Be judicious when placing a bet. Remember, if there is no expectation, there is little disappointment.

57. Unfortunately, sometimes, credit earned and credit deserved might be too much for others to concede.

58. Personal aspirations do not require validation or acceptance by others.

59. While you cannot stop someone from talking, you can stop yourself from listening.

CHAPTER 8

MY THOUGHTS

*"The world as we have created it is a process of our thinking.
It cannot be changed without changing our thinking."*
—Albert Einstein

Twoscore, one decade, nine years! That is me today, at age 59. Within two months of the time of this writing, God willing, my time here can be succinctly expressed as "threescore." An incomprehensible phrase, label, and age that I was incapable of visualizing a brief one score ago.

The time and space I've occupied feel like an eternity that moved at the speed of light. Now, I can see my event horizon, or at least have become fully aware of what *The End* really means. Fortunately, I'm a lot more of my now and a lot less of my then. Evolution is the change in the characteristics of a species over several generations. For me, the cadence of time's pendulum has been ticking much quicker. I evolved with each decade and realized the next major step is two months away.

I am anxiously awaiting to see more of the new me. What follows in this chapter are just tidbits of what I have learned from life and who I've become. Caution: I remain a work in progress.

BECOMING

I don't fully understand exactly what is going on. But I'm now wise enough not to question what or why it continues to happen with increased clarity and intensity. Instead, I have chosen to let it flow and avoid trying to figure it out. I've learned that some things are simply beyond my capacity to comprehend. In the end, the final product is not of my doing but a gift given to me. I'm not sure how much longer I will receive them. So time is of the essence.

I have developed a great respect for this new process; it is enlightening. I anxiously await the moment when the ocean pulls old sand away from a now-familiar beach. I know my role: open my mind and tamper down my instincts. Let humble and reflective thoughts create words, sentences, and paragraphs from my fingertips.

Do not worry; there will be time for minor editing when the dust settles. And yes, I'll know precisely when the burst for this special musing has been extinguished. I have faith in the new self I am becoming and being. My iCloud now leverages a portfolio with 59 years of burnished lessons. I trust this uncomfortable thought evolution. The results tend to speak for themselves and might speak on behalf of others. Perhaps it will speak volumes about the humbling confidence in the perpetual, enduring power of hope now emerging from me.

IN ME

We all have quirks and unique habits, little things that we have done instinctively throughout our lives. Those who know you can quickly identify you by subtle but distinct mannerisms and phrases. So much so that, if given a few arbitrary data points in a single-blind study, much like a seasoned detective, they could piece together a profile and, with a high degree of confidence, declare, "I think I've solved the case. I'm pretty sure I know who this is!"

Have you ever wondered why you do some of the things you do? Why do you latch onto certain things, people, and causes? Well, after 59 years, I'm finally starting to understand why and how I am who I am. Why I've always been meticulous, organized, even-keeled, quiet, a collaborator, inclusive, an observer, a peacemaker, and a documenter.

I can confidently say that something not of this earth, an intuitive presence, has been there from my beginning, blessing me, guiding me, molding me, testing me, and preparing me for this very moment today. This presence has been patiently waiting to see if and when I would connect the dots, so they could finally assess the return on their investment in me.

SOMETHING

Everyone has a story to tell. Some are just beginning their journey; others are reaching the trail's end. At some point, each of us will have our own "something" to overcome. No one gets out of this thing we call life unscathed, but we can share life lessons and break the trail for others.

When we speak about who we are and what we've gone through, it's akin to reading a book's preface, but it's more important to look at someone's entire body of work. It's there that the content, style, and merit can best be evaluated. Often the preface is an aspirational state and out-of-reach. After calibration, you'll know if the story should be classified as fiction or non-fiction.

If you have already embraced your "something," I encourage you to do something with it. Share it with others who are going through their own challenges and those currently in denial. Help them understand, it's not the weight of the load but how you carry the burden. When their "something" comes, the seeds of your inspirational advice can bear nourishing and comforting fruit.

There is no benefit in taking your "something" into eternity. It is far better to leave as many gifts here on earth as possible. Some will be opened shortly, and others long after you are gone. So leverage the light given to you now to illuminate the path for others in the future.

VULNERABLE LEADERSHIP

Too many leaders get caught up thinking about their power rather than their responsibility to those they lead. Yet in all leadership roles, there is an informal dependence on others. In many ways, that reliance is more critical than the power or authority implied by one's placement at the top of an organizational chart.

One key component of leadership often overlooked and rarely discussed is vulnerability. Vulnerability is uncertainty, risk, and emotional exposure. It is not a sign of weakness; it can be a confident leader's greatest strength. Vulnerability is not winning or losing; it's having the courage to show up and be seen when leaders have no control over the outcome. This is true courage, which is precisely what a team and organization need from its leader during times of uncertainty.

In the end, it's not about the leader. It's about a relationship between them, and the individuals challenged to help transform something good into something great if you sincerely want to build organizational trust, respect, honesty, and creativity. Most leaders already possess the necessary tools. Just remember to lead by example with confidence, integrity, and vulnerability.

THE GIFT OF LIFE

This week I celebrated a milestone event. It's an important stop along my journey that I would have avoided at all costs if given a choice. Emotionally, physically, and psychologically, I now realize I am stronger after fully embracing it. This is my "something." Everybody's got at least one. If they don't right now, as my Aunt Babe always says, "Baby, just keep on living."

It's a no-frills routine. First, I check-in 15-20 minutes before my appointment, take a seat, and wait patiently, periodically checking my phone for business emails. Then, when my name is called, I grab my computer bag, greet my host, and walk down a sterile hallway and into a familiar room with familiar smells and familiar faces.

I make a point to greet everyone I encounter while simultaneously looking for an empty window seat. A view outside and at the clouds is a good distraction from the events about to take place. The same is true, at least for me if I'm on a plane. OK, I found it. I set my laptop bag down, grab my Gatorade Zero and set it on the pull-up side table. I pull out my laptop, log in, and relax into the familiar recliner.

I catch up with the nurses while they meticulously complete standard prep protocols. "Where is Amanda?"Did she finally move to Houston?" "I thought you said you were going to play some of your music?" It takes the edge off the situation for them and everyone sitting in the same position as me. I look around and can see a few smiles. That was for us.

Then my three-hour rejuvenation begins. Again. But this time, there is something slightly different. Today is a special day, or so I was told. I am about to begin my 100th session. These sessions have been performed without fail every six weeks since 2009, with one exception—January of 2021.

Being a bit of a nerd, I was caught off guard when hearing of this centennial event. I paused and didn't know if I should be happy, sad, or amazed for a brief second. I silently chastised myself, "You should have captured that data on a spreadsheet and known about this." But after 12 years, I lost track of just how many intravenous Remicade infusions have taken place. They've become a routine part of my life. I would not be alive today without this minor inconvenience. Others would love to be in my shoes.

A lifelong treatment regimen that helps keep me alive. So it's a special gift, not a milestone, that I am genuinely thankful to have received.

MAKING A LIVING VS. MAKING A LIFE

Work is something that I do, but it is not who I am. It does not define what is at my core. It's just what I have to do to survive. A job, a position, my career. I've continuously poured everything into it because that's how I was raised, and besides, my effort is my brand. And that is where the opposites begin to attract. This thing we call "work" is a small but essential part of life.

Over time, things have slowly changed. Now, I am fortunate to be in a position to say, "I love what I do," because I make my own choices, and I have the final say.

I make a concerted effort to engage those industries that I value most and whose values align closely with mine. I am now investing my remaining time and energy attempting to impact healthcare, pharmaceuticals, biotechnology, life sciences, nonprofits, and other organizations that save or improve the quality of people's lives.

A beam of light now permeates through my mind, body, and soul, as many have confirmed, exclaiming, "Man, you look so at peace, relaxed, and confident." After 59 years, when I look in the mirror, I have to concur. I guess I am peaceful, relaxed, and confident now.

Over time, the gap between what I do and who I am has all but vanished. Those disparate lines have completely blurred into one that strategically converges around people, relationships, and impact. As a result, I am a better person and grateful for this evolution. I am excited, anxious, and blessed each day I awake.

THE SANDS OF TIME

Looking back on life, there are many moments I wish I could have accelerated through, and others I long to revisit, but this time at a snail's pace. So today, I try to leverage my life lessons to optimize the remaining grains of sand left in my hourglass.

In the best-case scenario, I have all but utilized at least three-fourths of my precious allotment. Worst case, well, there is no value in trying to guess the exact date of my fate. The chronographic permutations are endless, sobering, and futile. And besides, the act of investing in that process uses more of the very thing we attempt to control: precious, unknown time.

The huge variable we all face is not knowing the exact time of our life event horizon. So we place our best bets on where, how, and with whom our time is allocated—knowing that this nonstrategic endeavor is severely flawed. Objects in the rearview mirror, by design dissipate with time and distance. Look ahead with positivity at the possibilities. Learn from mistakes, learn to forgive yourself, learn from others, and live life to the fullest.

Time waits for no one. Its constant vibrations slowly sift away precious moments of your life like grains of sand until there is nothing left. It is a non-retrievable asset, so use it wisely.

GOSPEL IN MY SOUL

Its origins were conceived from the pain, suffering, and oppression of its people, but today, gospel music is universally shared, heard, sung, and recognized. It now plays a prominent role in religious settings and is performed for many purposes, including aesthetic pleasure, ceremonial purposes, and as a sacred entertainment product in the global marketplace.

I can instinctively recall the words and melodies to certain gospel songs without having heard them for over fifty years. They remind me of places of worship, revered elders, dear friends, and congregation members no longer here, but through gospel music, they live on forever because of this music. I guess those old spirituals touched my spirit. There are certain songs by certain people that I leverage in certain situations. Here are a few that might be of use to you someday.

STRENGTH: *I Need You Now* (Smokie Norful); *Near The Cross* (Dorothy Norwood); *Precious Lord* (Sister Rosetta Tharpe); *Pass Me Not* (Billy Preston)

GRATEFULNESS: *Amazing Grace* (Mahalia Jackson); *Still Amazed* (Full Gospel Baptist Church); *What a Friend* (Aretha Franklin); *Oh Happy Day* (Bebe & Debbie Winans)

HOPE & FAITH: *Jesus Is Love* (The Commodores); *Old Time Religion* (Bishop Leonard Scott) *Still I Rise* (Yolanda Adams) *Precious Memories* (Sister Rosetta Tharpe)

TRANSITIONING & DEATH: *Going Up Yonder* (Tremaine Hawkins); *Take Me to the King* (Tamela Mann); *Walk Around*

Heaven (Patti LaBelle); *Somewhere Around the Throne* (The Mighty Clouds of Joy)

From Black American churches to the Grammy Awards, gospel music is a touchstone of American culture. So I felt it was only appropriate to end this chapter with solemn grace and personal reflection. It's a nice segue into the *59 Prime*'s final chapter, **My Hope**.

CHAPTER 9

MY HOPE

"Hope is being able to see that there is light despite all the darkness."—Desmond Tutu

Each day is a special day, a new one that none of us has ever witnessed before. A day that, unfortunately, some individuals will never get a chance to experience. So the question is, will you approach it in the same way that that you have every other day thus far? If you have been contemplating making a minor tweak or trying a different approach, try this: say "Hi" to someone that you haven't before or have been meaning to, simply offer a kind word of support, encouragement, or recognition.

It takes just as long NOT to say something as it does TO say something uplifting. The only difference is the potential return on those fleeting 5-10 seconds of your investment.

119

Oh, and if you don't have the opportunity today, no worries, this type of effort does not have an expiration date. But sooner is better than later, as most of us are procrastinators when it comes to change. Time does not.

We are given a different but finite amount of time here to spread our wings and soar. Never let anyone stifle your flight. I believe it's imperative to understand those who are adding or extracting value from life. For those who unintentionally extract value, quickly give them feedback and a chance to recalibrate accordingly. For those who intentionally extract value, quickly provide them with the gift of feedback, wish them well, and immediately purge. Make room for much-needed sunshine, positivity, and value-adding relationships and experiences.

Your prime might occur earlier or later than mine did. The scars could be more profound. The reflections are more traumatic. Life events resonate and cascade upon each of us differently. Yet, sharing our life experiences, both good and bad, can light a clearer path for others. That simple act of giving can be a blessing, a ray of hope, and a part of your legacy.

Some will read *59 Prime* and instantly "get it," no further explanation required. I am not so sure why it took me so long to arrive at this point. But I'm incredibly proud to be here. There were more unanticipated twists, climbs, valleys, and rivers to cross than I ever imagined. But now, I have finally arrived and "thank them for leaving the light on."

If you are willing, try to be the type of person who never meets a stranger, and couple that with a mindset to treat people like you want to be treated. I promise you: your life will be enriched, more fulfilling, and impactful. You'll grow organically and spiritually because of the incredible people you meet along your journey, and the collective lessons you will learn from them and about yourself.

Life is circular. The ancient Chinese philosophy of yin-yang ☯ has merit. Life is incredibly non-dualistic, meaning that there is something in everything. In the good, there is bad, and in the bad, there is good. In the end, everything in life has balance. Find yours and relish it.

My 59th year has been one of awakening. May you find peace, happiness, and your own prime in this life. When you do, pay it forward, don't take it with you. It could be an inspiring and lifesaving gift to someone known or unknown.

My roots, path, headwinds, and journey have refined my life priorities. Up until now, you've heard nothing about politics for a good reason, as it means very little to me. I do not care about politics or your political affiliation. If you treat all people equally and with respect, that is what matters to me. I'm a pretty good judge of character, primarily because I watch what people do versus what they say—especially those entrusted with leadership positions, power, or influence.

After being hospitalized three times, I realized what a blessing those events were for me. I was given the precious gift of time alone to reflect and contemplate the things in life that were important to me, things that I missed the most at that moment, and things that I would likely miss in my final days. So I made a promise to devote the majority of my time and energy to those things, which primarily revolved around my T5. Not surprisingly, politics did not make the cut; it was not even on my radar screen.

History has shown that politics is one of the few things in life where hypocrisy, greed, and discrimination are inextricable, perpetual, and oscillating byproducts. The plain, simple truth is that it's just not something I inquire about or care to discuss. That is my official political position and affiliation. I will not devote more than one paragraph to it as proof of its lack of relevance in my life.

My professional life, like pieces of a familiar puzzle, has fallen back into place. I say that, knowing nothing happens by chance, but instead because of Divine Providence.

I relaunched BEAM Executive Advisors in late August, and began notifying my network that I was "back in the game." Through referrals, I was having exploratory engagement conversations with two CEOs, a CHRO, and municipal board members by early September. By late September, all four were officially clients. I remain genuinely blessed. It's as if my seven-month detour took me off the highway and onto the access road to slow things down. Three of these companies are in industries that provide products and services that significantly improve and save people's lives. This is where I prefer to spend my professional time, experience, and energy. It's self-motivating and noble work: what a blessing and further confirmation of Divine Providence.

Because of **My Roots, Path**, and **Journey**, I believe I operate at my best when things appear to be at their worst. At 59, I am more thankful, humble, caring, inclusive, and optimistic.

Reflectively, 2021 has been a year of dramatic changes in my life. How I think, engage and react, and how, where, and with whom I spend my remaining and unknown allotment of time is of the utmost importance to me.

Somehow, I quietly and solemnly faced three OR anesthesia surgeries, two non-anesthesia optical laser surgeries, a four-day "in-patient," high-dose steroid infusion, and absorbed close to five thousand milligrams of life-saving Prednisone… not exactly what I envisioned while bringing in the New Year.

Undoubtedly, 2021 was incredibly different from any of my previous 58 years. But I also know that right now, millions of people around the globe have or are enduring significant life challenges. They too have a story to tell, with even more powerful evidence of Divine Providence and the intrinsic power of the human spirit.

Whatever 2022 and beyond brings, I have new tools to draw upon: experiences, faith, and confidence. So, for that and 2021, I am eternally grateful. After all, it was 2021 that inspired me to write *59 Prime.*

Remember, in the twinkling of an eye, things can and will change. So ask yourself, when the dust settles, what will you have done with this precious gift of life?

59 Prime is my first attempt to share an inspirational message about my life experiences and potentially leave something of post-mortem value. Please pray for me, as I will continue to do so for you. Learn from your mistakes and experiences, but do not dwell on them. There's a reason that the rearview mirror is small, and the windshield in front of you is large. There are brighter days ahead. Together, we can make this world a better place.

Stay safe, be kind, and remain blessed.
Sincerely,
Michael K. Francis
December 2021
Website: www.59Prime.com   Email: michael@59prime.com

AFTERWORD

I have had the fortune of knowing Michael (aka Mikey just to me) for over 43 years from a personal stance; I married into the family of love 41 years ago to his brother Tony. At the time, I was the only sister-in-law in the family, and as time went on, I felt closer to being a sister than an in-law.

Michael has always been compassionate, humble, kind, and generous with a loving spirit, to name a few of his characteristics. He is very passionate about mankind; he always says, "Just treat people right because it's the right thing to do." His daily walk is a prime example of his character, and it says everything one needs to know about the person he is.

One day Mike and I were talking, and he began sharing with me unexplainable forces he was experiencing, driving him to write down poignant thoughts that were coming to mind at random times of the day and night, sometimes for hours at a time. He started out writing thoughts on post-it notes. In other conversations we had, Mike shared he could not sleep at times because the driving forces were so powerful. As the forces became increasingly stronger and stronger, he was experiencing a supernatural spiritual encounter with God and was chosen to share life's experiences he has encountered over time with others, giving them Hope. Mike continued to be obedient to his calling; as a result, we're blessed with *59 Prime*.

I love you Mikey, and thank you for being obedient!

Marilyn

Character: Who we are when no one is looking. It is making the tough decisions to act with integrity and trust when it costs us.

My dear friend and business colleague, Michael Francis, epitomizes the utmost of character and an open, teachable spirit. During the darkest days of the pandemic in 2021, when he was smitten with multiple health afflictions, including almost going blind, he did not blame others or utter, "Why me?" Instead, he humbly embraced the journey by leveraging the strength from his faith, roots, and headwinds. Join me in reading Michael's story of severe trial, near defeat, resilience, and openness to the power of hope, resiliency, and the message God had for him. This story will bless you as few overcomer stories will because it's written right from Michael's heart. *59 Prime* will enrich how you think about the past, present, and future as you go through some of your darkest moments.

Tom Garrett
Career CFO, Consultant, and Executive Coach

An epilogue serves as a comment or conclusion to a story. My comment is, Mike's book is the beginning of him being, as the old folk says, "grown." The ending to his story is being lived every day with many twists and turns to come.

The experiences he shares have helped advance the careers of the young people and seasoned professionals in our family, the village of friends, and others who asked. His knowledge of dealing with people, corporations, and himself speaks well to the future generations coming into the workforce.

In *The Maxims and Reflections of Goethe*, Johann Wolfgang von Goethe says, "He is the happiest man who can set the end of his life in connection with the beginning." I'm positive Mike's epilogue, when it arrives, will reflect this.

Cheryl Jefferson
Michael's Sister-In-Law

CPSIA information can be obtained
at www.ICGtesting.com
Printed in the USA
LVHW082132220222
711769LV00030B/682